CRAFTSCIT

The role and potential of the Crafts to economy,
employment and environment

Symposium papers presented
at the Showroom Cinema
Sheffield, UK
2nd March 1999

Ed. Dr. Hilary Cunliffe-Charlesworth

Acknowledgements:

Thanks should be made to the staff of the Crafts Council, and especially Stephen Burroughs; Jeremy Lampson of Design and Publishing for the Web, John Hardwick Associates, Ron Charlesworth; the staff of the Showroom Cinema especially Janet Laycock and Jay Arnold; and to colleagues at Sheffield Hallam, especially Chris Jones, Pat Watson, David Ball and Simon Quinn.

Sheffield Hallam University Press
Learning Centre
City Campus
Pond Street
Sheffield S1 1WB

First published 1999

Designed and typeset by Design Studio, Learning Centre, Sheffield Hallam University

©1999 ISBN 0 86339 862 6

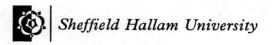 *Sheffield Hallam University*

CONTENTS

Foreword

Professor Elaine Thomas

The following papers were first presented before an audience from schools, from further education, from higher education, from the public sector, local authorities, small businesses and, importantly, practitioners.

I would like to emphasise that this is the audience whose commitment and contacts can help to make things happen for the crafts. The symposium presented a wide and impressive range of topics and an opportunity for each of the delegates to approach the issues from a different perspective. This creative synergy engendered new ideas and provided a forum within which new developments could emerge.

I was pleased that the event was hosted in Sheffield, as the crafts, indeed art and design generally, is very important to the city and to the region. As Director of the School of Cultural Studies at Sheffield Hallam University, I am committed, as are the staff, to the contribution that creativity can make to both the quality of life and to the economy of the nation and the region, and I think that in this context we must clarify and enhance the status and meaning of the term "crafts". I'm sure that these symposium papers will make a major contribution and I trust that you will all find it both stimulating and worthwhile.

2

Tracey Heyes, detail of ceramics, Sheffield Peace Gardens
© Sheffield Hallam University

Introduction

Dr. Hilary Cunliffe-Charlesworth

The Craftscity symposium confirmed that we have a vibrant and productive Crafts industry. The papers contained in this book are as diverse and energetic as the people who attended. They look at examples of practice; explore the opportunities for the Crafts and provide information on a range of issues. They reflect the breadth and depth of experience of the contributors: most papers remain little changed, while those who made less formal presentations are represented by edited transcripts or a reappraisals submitted after the symposium. The papers were illustrated with images of the projects discussed, but this book can only provide a selection.

The Crafts industry has been recognised as an essential element of the National economy since the 1980s but its role has never been clearly acknowledged or defined. However, we do know the creative sector is a part of the economy which is expanding, and that between 1991 and 1996 this sector was growing nationally at a rate of 17.5%.

In the Yorkshire and Humberside region, where this symposium was held, the growth rate is only some 7.2%. and this highlights the importance of encouraging micro industries in a region where skilled labour was once crucial in the development of heavy industry, in order to ensure a sound economic future. A number of initiatives have been instigated to develop the cultural industries here, often drawing on the experiences of European partners, and providing examples of good practice. It is recognised that in many such projects, Design and the allied role of Craft play a key role in improving the existing environment, as well as the development of new areas for employment and addressing the needs for leisure.

Yorkshire is to be designated a European Centre for Design Excellence: an initiative for research funded by the Design Council and regional TEC's under the title Networking for Industry. Certainly as a region Yorkshire can demonstrate a diversity of approach to the inclusion of crafts: from architecture, by building on traditional artisan/craft skills; though developing contemporary visions of how modern craft today can engage with industry; and even to exploring new markets for the Crafts. Many of the region's business and public sector organisations are already empowered and aware, and, as can be seen in the following papers, a range of practical initiatives demonstrate collaborative or shared goals between all levels of education, the public sector, and commerce and industry are taking place. What needs to be done is to communicate the problems; solutions, and successes, especially so with the shift from the centrality of the Crafts Council to a more devolutionary approach.

Through these papers we can see how the Crafts are having a direct impact: on learning new craft skills and improving and adapting these skills. These papers also demonstrate how the growth of industrial and educational networks and the use of craft designers with commercial partners are developing a policy which may impact on educational establishments and even more on regional frameworks.

A number of studies have been made on the impact of cultural policy on the economy: and the Yorkshire region has been at the forefront of such developments aware that its manufacturing base, once centred on heavy industry no longer requires the same number of employees and that service industries do not develop an economy which is production rich. It is hoped that this symposium will encourage a sharing of information and statistical evidence, to demonstrate the importance of Crafts for the future.

Industry is pollutant rich, and the concern for clean air and a healthy environment is a key issue. How green are the Crafts and to what extent can the Crafts demonstrate the principal of less meaning more? Can Crafts have a direct environmental impact? The Crafts are about the environment and respect for it.

For many the loss of heavy industry means a loss of regional identity. The current swing to devolution in Britain's political institutions is mirrored across Europe. There is a conflict between devolution and internationalisation of market boundaries. While the service industry of shopping has provided considerable employment for the Crafts our retailing centres are a demonstration of the 'McDonald-isation' of culture; and the 'IKEA-isation' of products which reflect a Craft ethos, made and marketed according to cultural segmentation and even reflecting ethnic designs of the third world.

Fortunately this region has deliberately planned for cultural industries. In 1991 the World Student Games triggered the construction of a range of facilities which incorporated public art, and this has been followed by other projects. The success or failure of the new Peace Gardens in Sheffield will stand on its commissioned projects. Projects which may be craft orientated but incorporate computer aided design and similar innovative technology for their completion. This project, and that of the Sheffield Millennium canteen, provide a base for discussion around issues on the function and purpose of public art, and the question of how effective Public Arts Officers are.

Among the collection is a paper noting the Persistence Works project, a new building to house workshops for a society of artists (not a cooperative). I well remember the concern of its members when the local authority originally set out its plans for the Sheffield Cultural Industries Quarter: this was perceived as a dangerous venture which would increase artists' rents and alienate an existing community of workers. Today contemporary Crafts are included in the Quarter, and perceived as one of its strongest constituents.

The term cultural industries (and even creative industries) is open to definition. For Sheffield the opening of the National Centre for Popular Music is the culmination of many years of optimistic planning, ensuring that policy makers hear the views of the wider majority, on what is included within 'the arts' framework; and the benefits to the economy of a wider group of participants, and a more universal and commercial focus.

The general perception of Crafts is very broad, and this would seem an appropriate time to draw together all sectors of education to ensure commonality of purpose and an understanding of the diverse issues we are facing. Education has to consider the needs of society and ensure its courses reflect the changing nature of employment, from full time, permanent contracts to part-time, temporary and freelance employment. For many working in the Crafts these work patterns have been accepted as the norm, but, education and the taxation and benefits systems need to consider their implications for the economy.

The Crafts have much to offer. They encourage the development of new tacit and practical skills, and the reskilling of blue collar workers. Such projects need funding and evaluating and are hindered by being small scale, driven by the needs of a local economy rather than national economic trends. Often, such projects fall under the remit of FE and Adult Education and Returning to Learning for this group of clients may mean something very different. Crafts at this level are not driven by aesthetics and theoretical debate, but by the economic needs of what can be produced with inexpensive materials and will sell successfully to customers who have little purchasing power.

Thus in part the Crafts have been marginalised by being perceived as backward looking (rather than innovative); concerned with heritage (rather than forging new styles and products) and produced by the sweat of artisans (brown rice and sandals) and how blue collar workers earn a wage (the Crafts for the middle classes are clean and produce objects for pleasure) or even part of healthcare (occupational therapy). Since the Crafts come from a tradition of working class skills or are produce of individualistic minds, I would suggest they have also been, and still are, marginalised in terms of research. In contemporary society the Crafts may be seen more appropriately as a series of micro economic groups, each providing economic benefits in terms of trade, employment and social cohesion.

We hope and trust that the contrasting views of the participants at the Craftscity symposium will lead to a lively debate and future cooperation. In one sense this symposium was valedictory, noting the passing of the Education Department of the Crafts Council and the reappraisal of structures supporting the Crafts. However, this symposium also can be seen as marking a new beginning for the Crafts: it was held in Sheffield, a city which demonstrates many of the positive attributes the Crafts bring to a community, and one of the delegates from the Sheffield Museums and Galleries Trust, Janet Barnes, has since been appointed as the Director of the Crafts Council.

We may only hope that the optimism of this symposium signals greater recognition for the role of Crafts, nationally and internationally.

Funding the Crafts –
Creating beyond traditional sources

Dr. Linda Moss

The current status of the crafts, is often perceived mainly by crafts people, designers and artists, to have a lower status, poorer access to funding, less influence on politics and policies for creative activity than do the so-called fine arts. But, I would argue that this perception is becoming outdated and that a more ambiguous status does have its advantages, particularly when funding is being sought.

The changing status: take for example the proposed amalgamation of the Crafts Council and the Arts Council for England. I have it from a senior source internal to the Arts Council that this won't be any kind of wholesale swallowing up of the Crafts Council. It may very well retain its own premises and staff and that is more likely to be like an exercise in contracting out of specialist services than a take over. If so, it is not in practice a money saving exercise. It is rather a statement about changing perceptions between the arts and the crafts, and a perception that it is inappropriate to maintain those historic distinctions. We can also see it as a further stage in a process which began with the shifting of the arts from domain of the office of Arts and Libraries which was an alliance which emphasised largely the educational section of the arts, and their segregation from other aspects of culture; to the creation of the rather quaintly named Department of National Heritage which brought together various branches of culture for the first time at government level. We now have the more realistically but cumbersomely titled Department of Culture, Media and Sports. Of course, on the surface these shifts are bureaucratic, but they both reflect and reinforce changing perceptions of the breath of what constitutes culture. This is only an official recognition of a trend which has been growing over the whole of the last half century, a decline in hierarchical ways in defining culture. I don't think this is the time or place to explore that trend but simply to note that it is there and that this is part of that process, and to note its impact on the status of the crafts.

Another reason why the status of the crafts is shifting is the new emphasis on creative industries. At a national level, at incipient regional level and local government levels, we can see a new emphasis on the importance of the cultural industries from Tony Blair's "think tank" and specially designated lottery funding. The crafts are a mainstay of this. We have designer/makers of all descriptions: fashion designers; those inventing new industrial and civic uses of traditional crafts material; all now seem to be contributing to economic growth and social change in a way which is beginning to eclipse the status of the fine arts. All this is recognised by those who are active in the crafts, and active in the cultural sector, but amongst officials who have no particular responsibility for culture, older prejudices often linger and it is these people who often control the allocation of funding for which the crafts could be eligible.

Some of these older attitudes can actually be advantageous in attracting money, because they give a better passport to non specific funding than the arts, and they are sometimes perceived as more approachable by the arbiters of non specific funding. Let me explain that in a little more detail. First, the availability of non specific funding which can be used by the crafts. There are lots of budgets which have no particular relevance for the crafts, for example the Single Regeneration Budget, English and Regional Tourist Board funds, the National Health Service, Local Government Economic Development funds in most local authorities and environmental funds. The crafts are not immediately identified as "arts" by those who determine the allocation of major European funds, and therefore tend to be eligible on social or economic rather than artistic criteria. It is not always even necessary to present your scheme or project as being crafts; it can be a rural economic development initiative, an environmental improvement, an ecological education project, or creating a healing atmosphere on a hospital ward. Because the crafts are perceived as closer than "the arts" to what is voluntarily practiced by lots of people in the community, non-cultural funders are more likely to be sympathetic to a crafts-based project in community activity than an arts project. This opens up a huge range of education and social budgets from local government and charitable trusts. This is not to argue that those perceptions are valid, simply that they exist and given that they exist, they may as well be harnessed them to the benefit of the crafts.

European Structural Fund, Objective 2 is a type of funding which is available for areas which have suffered from industrial decline, and South Yorkshire is one of these. So any project based locally it is likely to eligible for Objective 2, ERDF (European Regional Development Fund) and European Social Fund budgets.

How do you find out about this? The priorities for spending this budget are detailed in what is called the Single Programming Document which is available from the Regional Government Office (which for Yorkshire is based in Leeds) and it is free. It is quite a difficult read but you can pick from it and find out whether your particular project is likely to be eligible. One of the priorities for spend is new employment opportunities. This includes culture, media and tourism employment and also community based small enterprises, so if you are setting up a small enterprise in the crafts with a strong community purpose or involvement, there is some chance that you will be eligible for that budget.

Another example, is European Objective 5B which is available in areas of rural deprivation including the Pennine Uplands. This is divided into measures, for instance, Measure 1.5 is for the financial support to encourage self employment and the development of small businesses and of that currently £196,000 was unspent in Spring 1999; or Measure 4.2 environmental protection which had in early 1999 over half a million pounds unspent. This raises the question of why are there fewer eligible applications than resources, it is not the way round we usually expect to find a funding situation. I think this is because of a lack of knowledge amongst potential applicants and a kind of folk culture that European funding is extremely difficult to access. A lack of knowledge about how to apply and, it must be faced, the cumbersome nature of the application process, the eligibility criteria and the required monitoring once the award is made are further difficulties. Some of us in this room have first hand knowledge of this, the monitoring of that does take a quite burdensome amount of time.

I will conclude by looking at a couple of examples, one of which tapped into some unusual funding, and one which did not. First of all, Ashworth Special Hospital, on Merseyside, is one of three secure hospitals in

England, which is for the containment and treatment of people with severe psychiatric disorders and who are a danger to society. It is in structure and appearance a high security prison. Project work was borrowed from Yorkshire Sculpture Park and placed in the grounds of Ashworth Special Hospital for a period of several months. It was then removed and there was a general demand from staff and patients that there should be something similar to replace it. A team of artists were brought in to work with patients, and they constructed their own version of the sculpture, it is made of papier mache, covered with plaster bandages with a sheath of fibreglass on the outside. This was funded ultimately through the Home Office, through the budget for special hospitals. So an extremely odd budget to support the creation of sculpture but nonetheless it happened.

My next example tells the opposite story and concerns an organisation called Cobblestone Designs which is a small enterprise employing two or three stone cutters, owned and managed by Maggie Howarth. She designs and constructs mosaic pavements to order for everyone from local authorities to, as she puts it, to the crowned Heads of Europe. She has paid for her own specialised workshop premises, machinery and forklift trucks on the hilltop in North East Lancashire where she lives. The whole enterprise is entirely eligible for an Objective 5B funding grant and it was my job a few years ago to encourage applications to this fund, but Maggie was not to be persuaded. The time involved and the need to broker a package of funding from a variety of sources (because you cannot have European money without partnership funding) and the intricacies of the monitoring process led her to take a purely commercial decision that her time was much more profitably spent on creative work than it was on devoting time to the attraction of funding.

So I think in conclusion we have to say that each enterprise must work out a rather cold blooded costing of its time in relation to the amount of funding needed. It is likely that new organisations are likely to find the ratio between time and funding more worthwhile, than well established businesses like Cobblestone Mosaics. But it is worth considering a wider range of funding than that which is available through conventional resources.

Funding the Crafts -
What is Available in the European Union

Dr. Nigel Mortimer

This paper examines, in particular, the possible funding opportunities which might occur for the Crafts under the Fifth Framework Programme (FP5) of the European Commission (EC). FP5 is currently the major mechanism for funding research and technological development (RTD), including demonstration, within the European Union (EU). There has been some suggestion that links could eventually be created between FP5 and European Structural Funds (ESF) which represent a very significant resource for economic and social development, and environmental improvement within the EU.

Although the relevance and availability of ESF are not the subject of this particular paper, it should be noted that, in future, this type of support will be governed by the principles described in "Sustainable Urban Development in the European Union: A Framework for Action" (COM/98/605: available via the Europa website on www.inforegio.cec.int/urban/forum/src/frame1). This extremely important document was officially launched by Directorate-General (DG) XVI of the EC at the European Urban Forum in Vienna, Austria, between 26 and 27 November 1998. The stated purpose of the Framework for Action is "to ensure that EC policies become more effective by better taking into account the potential of urban areas and the challenges facing them".

The emphasis on urban areas is important since this is the intended future target for the majority of funding within the EU. However, further details of ESF can be found elsewhere. It is the main concern of this paper to address funding opportunities under FP5, especially from the perspective developed by the "City of the Future" Inter-Sectoral Platform, which is an established EU-wide network of urban stakeholders committed to sustainable urban development and management. From this perspective, numerous important opportunities for funding the Crafts from FP5 can be identified and elaborated.

The Fifth Framework Programme (FP5) was officially launched at a major conference in Essen, Germany, on 25 and 26 February 1999. It is a five year programme of RTD funding, which will extend from 1998 to 2002, with a total budget of Euro 14,960 million (further details can be obtained through the official website www.cordis.lu/fp5). Unlike previous RTD programmes, FP5 will concentrate on significant problem-solving RTD activities. In particular, a central theme of FP5 will be the creation, application and dissemination of solutions which meet the needs of EU citizens. Hence, key objectives are economic competitiveness and social well-being, with particular attention to employment, environmental improvement and enhancement of quality of life.

It is specifically in relation to this last issue that opportunities for the Crafts can be set. In general terms, FP5 will consist of three horizontal programmes and four thematic programmes of RTD funding. The horizontal programmes are generic in nature and cut across themes to provide assistance in general areas, including "Confirming the International Role of Community Research" (Euro 475 million), "Promotion of Innovation and Encouragement of Small- and Medium-sized Enterprises" (Euro 363 million) and "Improving Human Research Potential" (Euro 1,280 million). In particular, this last horizontal programme will provide funding for training and mobility of researchers. Hence, as previously, support will exist for researchers in many fields to take part in exchange arrangements involving institutions, organisation and companies in other EU member states.

The four thematic programmes within FP5 consist of "Quality of Life, Management of Living Resources" (Euro 2,413 million), "User-Friendly Information Society" (Euro 3,600 million), "Competitive and Sustainable Growth" (Euro 2,705 million), and "Energy, Environment and Sustainable Development" (Euro 1,083 million). It will be appreciated that, given the intentionally holistic problem-solving emphasis of FP5, no single thematic programme specifically addresses issues related only to the Crafts. Instead, it can be seen that opportunities may exist for the Crafts within a number of thematic programmes.

However, such opportunities can only be realised successfully if the skills encompassed within the Crafts are combined in a complementary manner with other technical and non-technical expertise to generate whole solutions to important problems which may be complex and challenging. Throughout FP5, it is recognised that serious problems require global and integrated approaches which require effectively co-ordinated multi-disciplinary effort. Additionally, proposed projects must have practical outcomes which can be applied to a number of EU member states or, ideally, across all EU members states. Hence, potential dissemination and replication are important aspects which will be expected in any good FP5 proposal. Because of these and other considerations, opportunities for the Crafts within FP5 must be developed in an innovative manner.

When calls for proposals are issued, it will be essential to study the RTD priorities carefully to identify such opportunities. Calls for proposals will be linked to specific Key Actions within each thematic programme. Relevant opportunities may arise within any Key Action. For example, the Key Action "Multimedia Content and Tools" (Euro 564 million) occurs within the thematic programme on the "User-Friendly Information Society". The stated aim of this Key Action is "to improve information products and services to enable linguistic and cultural diversity". By combining Crafts knowledge with Information Technology (IT) expertise, suitable projects for funding might be formulated which "expand the contribution of libraries, museums and archives to the emerging culture economy".

The Key Action on the "City of Tomorrow and Cultural Heritage" (Euro 170 million) within the thematic programme on "Energy, Environment and Sustainable Development" is probably the most relevant part of FP5 for the Crafts. The principal objective of this Key Action is "to support sustainable economic development and competitiveness, improved urban management and integrated planning policy, and help safeguard and improve the quality of life and cultural heritage of citizens". DG XII is responsible for this particular Key Action and the relevant EC official is Dr. David Miles.

One particular RTD priority within this Key Action is the "protection, conservation and enhancement of European cultural heritage" which is intended to "develop sound management of cultural resources of cities and urban regions to improve citizens' quality of life, tourism and job creation". Prior to the first call for proposals on this Key Action, the purpose of this RTD priority seems to have been mainly interpreted in terms of the technologies which can assist with the preservation of culturally-important buildings. Hence, there appears to be some emphasis on "technologies for the diagnosis, protection, conservation, restoration and sustainable exploitation of historic buildings, museums, libraries and artifacts". However, broader opportunities may arise for the Crafts, depending on subsequent elaboration of this RTD priority.

For example, the "integration of cultural heritage into the urban setting" has been identified previously as a relevant topic area for RTD funding. The meaning of this potential topic area can be translated in many different ways. However, one exciting and ambitious possibility is that it could cover planning, development and management procedures for reviving historical centres in EU towns and cities that are in danger of becoming "tourist exhibits" by regenerating them as "living and working" cultural environments. Such cultural re-development would stress the need to preserve the historical content of an area whilst simultaneously promoting the sympathetic creation of suitable housing, business premises, urban infrastructure and amenities. This approach would attract local citizens back into such areas where they become a vital components of the community, economy and ambience.

Another challenging RTD priority has been referred to as the "sustainable exploitation of, and sustainable access to cultural heritage". The problem suggested by this priority is that the very popularity of certain examples of cultural heritage may lead to their degradation and destruction by the shear number of people who wish to visit them. This is a typical dilemma which may be partly resolved by the development of IT techniques such as virtual reality which would enable many people to gain some visual experience of cultural heritage at locations remote from the actual site. Although this would not replace actual experience of visiting a site, it might reduce some of the pressures on popular locations by encouraging more selective tourism.

Additional opportunities may arise for the Crafts in a very prominent RTD priority which deals with the sustainable development of cities through refurbishment and renovation. To achieve sustainability, existing buildings must be come more efficient in their use of all natural resources, especially energy. Concern over the adverse impacts of global climate change, reflected in the internationally-agreed Kyoto Protocol, mean that carbon dioxide emissions from the combustion of fossil fuels, as the world's current main sources of energy, must be reduced. As buildings account for a very substantial proportion of total carbon dioxide emissions in the EU, improved energy efficiency and greater use of renewable sources of energy are important parts of the response to this problem. This presents a major challenge for relevant professions, including those from the Crafts, who are charged with developing practical and replicable refurbishment and renovation techniques which introduce energy efficiency improvements and renewable energy technologies, such as passive and active solar energy measures, whilst preserving the architecture integrity and quality of these buildings.

Probably the most crucial stage in the preparation of a proposal for EC is the call for proposals. The reason for this is that the call will give clear indications about the types of proposal which are actually being encouraged at that point in time. However, basic preparations prior to the call should not be overlooked. It has already been stressed in pre-launch events for FP5 that those who intend to respond to calls for proposals should "prepare to participate now, or it may be too late". This means that currently-available information on the aims, objectives and priorities of FP5 should be studied and initial project concepts should be formulated accordingly. This will enable proposers to develop the fundamental features of their proposal and begin the vital process of searching for relevant partners.

The first calls for proposals are expected in March 1999, although some slippage is not unlikely. Not every aspect of FP5 will be covered by the first calls. Instead, calls will occur at intervals so that each RTD priority within the thematic and horizontal programmes is addressed in a realistic and systematic manner. Based on previous experience, the time between a call and the deadline for submission of proposals may be about three months. To assist with the development of high-quality proposals, which are emphasised by the EC, a pre-proposal checking service will be available. Proposers will be able to submit a brief outline of their proposal concept (no more than two sides of A4 paper) to designated staff within the relevant DG. It has been proposed that a response will be provided within five working days of receipt of the outline. The response will indicate whether the outline is relevant to the specific purpose of that call for proposals.

Another important feature of the organisation of FP5 which is intended to assist the submission of high-quality proposals is that the criteria used by official evaluators to assess proposals will be published so that proposers themselves can check the relevance of their proposals. Eventual submission can be on either paper or electronic versions of the official proposal forms. Once an initial proposal concept has been formulated, it is extremely important that its details are developed further in relation to the requirements and format of the official proposal form. Typically, this process is the responsibility of the lead partner who completes the form in consultation with other members of the partnership. Unless all the issues raised in these forms can be addressed fully and clearly, then a great deal of time and effort can be wasted in preparing a proposal which may be irrelevant to the EC.

Obviously, experience in the preparation of EC proposals can be a great advantage, especially given the relatively low success rates which can occur in particularly popular calls where the number of proposals submitted greatly exceed the number that can be supported. However, it can seem impossible to gain appropriate experience without first achieving success with a project proposal. Two strategies can be adopted to resolve this problem.

The longer-term solution is to develop experience of the selection procedures and an understanding of the features which make a good proposal by working for the EC as an official evaluator. Paid evaluators are always in demand by the EC although potential conflicts of interest must be avoided. The shorter-term answer may be to join existing partnerships, possibly as a minor partner, so that experience can be derived from subsequent involvement in a successful proposal. However, this can usually only be achieved if contacts with lead partners are already established and there is an existing relationship based on a mutual appreciation of the skills and expertise offered by each party. Such skills and expertise must be complementary and meet the needs of the proposed project. An existing track record of collaborative activity can assist the development of a relevant partnership.

Alternatively, both official and independent networks can be used to find suitable partners. A partner search service will also be provided through CORDIS, the Community Research and Development Information Service. The CORDIS FP5 Web Service (website address: www.cordis.lu/fp5) will provide the means to submit the details of specific "Expressions of Interest" (EoI) either electronically or on a paper-based form.

Clearly, any successful proposal is likely to be innovative and imaginative. However, practicality is also a central consideration for FP5 which will concentrate on integrated projects that combine required skills and expertise in an effective and complementary manner to provide appropriate solutions to important EU issues. Hence, there is emphasis on multi-disciplinary teams and, in order to promote practical projects of direct relevance to EU citizens, it is expected that major stakeholders will be involved in project proposals. Within the context of the "City of Tomorrow and Cultural Heritage" Key Action, local authorities are likely to play a prominent role in any project partnership. Normally, it will be expected that partnerships will consist of at least two partners from different EU member states.

The proposed project must not duplicate existing RTD work and it must demonstrate European added-value. In other words, the project must produce deliverables which have clear benefits to more than one EU member state. Ideally, the project should have wider potential throughout the EU. Hence, it must contain a practical mechanism for disseminating the positive results it produces. Additionally, a realistic way of replicating subsequent good practice should form part of the project plan. Consequently, the importance of trans-European networks should be apparent, not only in terms of creating a suitable partnership to undertake the work but also in relation to disseminating and replicating the outcomes of the project.

Obviously, the demands of FP5 are challenging. Projects must be "realistic but ambitious". They must have practical work programmes which can actually complete stated deliverables within a clear timescale and the funded budget. Most importantly, they must be capable of satisfying all the criteria required by the EC so that the aims and objectives of FP5 can be achieved. Despite the pressing demands of FP5, there will be numerous opportunities to develop and undertake an exciting range of diverse projects which will have significant social outcomes for the EU by contributing to economic competitiveness and social well-being. The many opportunities for the Crafts to participate will only be constrained by the limits of creative imagination.

The European Experience

Arcade Project, Finland
Eija Tanninen and Mirja Kälviäinen

The criteria for developing EU-projects within the Kuopio Academy of Crafts and Design, Finland is that they should centre on issues related to the Academy's research and development plan. This criteria is considered important because it guarantees the continuity of the project after the EU-funding has ended, and in addition ensures the expertise and commitment required by the project. Furthermore, many EU-funded projects are aimed at local development and sustainability, and should therefore cover issues considered important to the regional SMEs taking part in the project.

Three areas of development were discussed as possible targets for the EU-projects during the initial planning stage in the year 1995. These were: the use of new technology in the crafts and design enterprises; material research (material libraries and the ecological viewpoint); and issues of usability and marketing related to consumer interaction with the project and its participants.

The aim was to produce resources for the use by the SMEs and also to increase the level of information accessible for students and practitioners within the Kuopio Academy of Crafts and Design. More general aims of innovative research activities and international expert networking were also taken into consideration.

In the first stage of planning, the idea had been to subdivide the three areas for development into different projects. However, following advise from a consulting firm, the decision was made to combine these areas into one larger project. This decision proved to be correct as the project was accepted. The combination of different areas gave the project flexibility, and sufficient scope to use outside experts for different purposes.

The Arcade Project is a quality and development project for small and medium-size companies hosted by the Kuopio Academy of Crafts and

Design. The project focuses on increasing the information technology and ecological know-how in the field of Crafts and Design. The Arcade Project is an ESR-funded Adapt community initiative project. It was started on 1 December 1997, and it will be completed by 31 December 2000.

The project was announced to almost 600 companies in the Savo (Kuopio) region. Twenty different companies were selected for the project as so-called pilot companies. In size these companies vary from one-person enterprises to businesses employing up to ten people on different fields of Crafts and Design production, publishing, education, design, and multimedia know-how.

The Arcade Project is in active co-operation with partners located in the German Handwerkskammer Bildungszentrum Münster and Akademie Gestaltung im Handwerk, the Austrian Verein Faktor 4+, the Italian CSEA European Training Center for Agroindustry, for the Environment and for Sustainable Development, and at the Polytechnic of Turin the Department of Architecture, and the Portuguese Cencal Centro de Formacáo Profissional para a Industria Ceramica.

The objectives of the Arcade Project are to increase profits for companies through added value gained from information technology and ecologically sound operations, and to help companies build new domestic and international contact networks. The grasp of information technology and the creation of new networks are especially important goals, as the companies involved in the project are located in a remote area of Europe and Finland. The results generated by the project will be used to create a model which the other companies in the field can use to boost their operations and gain added value and efficiency in their business operations through information technology and ecological know-how.

The Arcade Project will also generate an electronic information service for the companies and professionals in the field. The information service is managed by the Taitemia Library of the Kuopio Academy of Crafts and Design, and it includes a materials bank about various materials and related innovations developed at the Academy of Crafts and Design, a directory of professionals and contacts, publications, and research material related to the field. Arcade studies the creation of an electronic materials, equipment, and machine exchange in the Internet, where companies could offer the excess materials and any equipment and machines in good condition for purchase by those who need them. The exchange is based on a net commerce system created in Arcade.

During the project, those companies which lacked computers and IT know-how, have been advised about the purchase of suitable equipment (a computer, a modem for the Internet connection, E-mail capability and a printer), and the entrepreneurs or other company personnel have been trained to use the computer. The project has arranged for a WWW domain for each company, and implements WWW sites for these companies. WWW sites consist of company information pages and a commerce system which has been created for companies involved in the Arcade project. The company WWW sites are implemented and produced in co-operation with the entrepreneur, a graphic designer, and a Web page programmer. When the company pages are finished, the company personnel are trained to handle the maintenance of both pictures and texts on these pages. A WWW site marketing brochure is produced for the companies.

Another task of Arcade is to help the project companies to locate planning and company management programs which support and facilitate the business operations, and to offer consultation and training about the use of the additional programs and equipment to the companies.

As this is being written, the project is at the halfway point. The entrepreneurs have been trained to use information technology, and the first net commerce pages for the companies have been finished by using the net commerce system developed in the Arcade project for Crafts and Design companies. The Arcade project publishes an electronic ecology guide for small and medium-sized companies called *Green Tips*, and a follow-up study has been started about the companies involved in the Arcade project. This study follows the company development during the project, and the success and failure points in the business of the project companies are examined.

The usability and marketing issues have been studied through development of design clinics with user feedback. Also some guides of consumer preference and usability issues will be published before the end of the project.

As result of the international co-operation, the Austrian Faktor 4+ will train Arcade entrepreneurs to ecologically sound thinking and measure the level of ecological soundness of Arcade companies during the spring of 1999. The German partners will arrange a project of their own for German entrepreneurs, and for the Finnish Arcade entrepreneurs, a joint Ecodesign workshop at Kuopio Academy of Crafts and Design in the Autumn of 1999. In the Spring of 2000 Arcade entrepreneurs will organise an Internet Business Show in Münster, Germany. This show will feature products and services by Arcade entrepreneurs, commerce via Internet, and a workshop about the experiences and future outlooks in the Internet commerce in the field.

The project does have some shortcomings. Even if one criterion for selection in the project was that the company's business strategy, production, marketing and logistics were in order, it would then have been necessary to examine the clarification of business strategy, marketing, and even product development. However, it was not possible to examine these issues within the project, and it would seem that after the termination of the Arcade project, some companies may require assistance in these areas.

As the commercial sites have been constructed, the most significant problem has been the creation of an electronic payment system, especially for foreign trade. It is still difficult for small companies to create a secure and easy payment system for their own site, as a uniform, international payment system does not exist.

The large amount of materials information to be included in the information service has made it difficult to convert the information in the electronic form. When the project was planned, we allocated insufficient time and labour resources for generation of materials banks.

After the project is finished, the most significant factor for companies is to link their net commerce pages to other net commerce sites and search engines. This linkage should support their business as efficiently as possible but it should also be sufficiently inexpensive. It is especially important to ensure that the net commerce sites and the electronic information service will be marketed.

Contact information

Eija Tanninen
The Kuopio Academy of Crafts and Design Arcade-project
tel:+358-17-308126, mobile:+358-50-5434268
fax:+358-17-308444

Craftworker, Clay Cross Adult Education Centre
© Simon Nadin

The importance of Crafts and Communities

Jane Glaister

I want to address the problem (as I see it) of the perception of crafts as a separate entity in our post-industrial society, and to look briefly at some of the ways that Rotherham (in its capacity as a Council) is trying to change this and ensure that crafts are on the agenda.

I recognise that to the general public crafts are "something our children do at school"; "beautiful products beyond the reach of most people's pocket" and "traditional pastimes". To local authorities, crafts, if they have a profile at all, are generally linked to economic regeneration, and specifically tourism; or an issue only for the education sector.

Craft products - and often the craftsmakers, are more isolated today from communities than at any other time in history. They are not just physically isolated, but emotionally isolated. Until the commercialisation and mass production of the industrial revolution craft makers were integral to the communities they worked in, supplying the needs of those people but, also defining and establishing the identity of those communities. They were not "separate" from their communities and nor did they "separate" themselves from other professions. Architects, craftsmen, landscape designers all worked together in the closest possible harmony each blending their styles and designs to produce a perfect whole.

Unless the role of crafts is understood, acknowledged and supported within a holistic framework - a framework which covers time and space; unless they are "reintegrated" into communities everyday life crafts will become even more "separate" and, thus, unsustainable other than in a voyeuristic, nostalgic way or as an aesthetic elite.

Local authorities can be a major inhibitor or a major promoter of the development of crafts within their area. They can be an inhibitor by treating them as "peripheral" - at best; they can be a major promoter if they recognise the role of crafts within, and throughout their whole agenda.

In 1998, Rotherham Metropolitan Borough Council launched its cultural strategy, after eighteen months of research, auditing activity and community consultation. The strategy recognises culture, in both its material and value dimensions, as central to the regeneration of the borough. It advocates the role of a "cultural continuum" ensuring linkages between school, community, further education, careers and lifelong learning. The Government is now requiring all local authorities to develop cultural strategies providing an opportunity for crafts development to be addressed properly at a local level. Within our very comprehensive cultural strategy sector specific plans are being developed and the Crafts Development Plan is primarily community focused.

Rotherham Borough is made up of many small towns and villages with a large rural area. The decimation of the coal and steel industries in the 1970s and 1980s have left many communities struggling to re-assert their identities and loss of confidence, a feeling of devalued skills and degraded environments are a significant issue. However, to impose things on these communities would exacerbate further a feeling of helplessness, so we choose to work <u>with</u> the communities.

In Rotherham we are just at the beginning of a process which attempts to reintegrate crafts with local communities. Firstly, by researching and raising awareness of the crafts "heritage" of specific communities. Examples are the heritage of fancy iron-work in Rotherham, stone masonry and stained glass in Laughton-en-le-Morthen, embroidery in the Kashmiri community, glass making in Catcliffe and pottery and porcelain in Swinton. I am not suggesting immediately resurrecting these crafts in these communities, but by developing an understanding and awareness of where crafts "fit" in the history of individual communities gives a legitimacy to crafts development work. Unemployment in the Borough is high, yet ex-steelworkers and coal miners have very high levels of "traditional craft skills" which can be re-directed to great effect (often by working with artists and designers) on projects which are relevant and beneficial to the communities and to the individuals for example: village signs where designs are facilitated by an artist working with the community and cast by ex-steelworkers; couture fashion produced by Kashmiri seamstresses working with a top couture designer. Secondly, by auditing existing skills in communities, and here I am referring to information at an individual level (but crafts, by definition is about individual skills), in order to be able to acknowledge, use and develop those skills. Thirdly, by using the vast purchasing power that we, as a local authority have, more creatively. We recently needed to replace the carpets in the foyer of Clifton Park Museum and instead of buying from the usual standard carpet suppliers we commissioned Pete Colgan to produce rugs for us (thanks to a grant from the Regional Arts Board this cost us no more than if we'd bought off the shelf). We are about to refurbish the library cafe and bar and shall be looking to crafts commissions rather than mass-manufacturers; the next time we need to replace the Town Hall crockery we shall look to crafts people rather than standard suppliers, and mirrors in our public lavatories have been commissioned from students at Rotherham College of Arts and Technology. This local authority "patronage" is very much a continuation of the "heritage" of crafts. The medieval crafts guilds were as much political as crafts based groupings selecting the mayor of their town and city from amongst their number.

Our biggest project at the moment is the Centenary Market development in the centre of Rotherham. Artist/Blacksmith, Andrew Smith, has been working, as part of the project team, on the design of security grilles, signage and gates. With technical advice from local steelworkers the grilles and gates will be both beautiful and functional and will be a true reflection of the steel-making heritage of the area. Managing the relationship between the architects, artist and community has been fraught with difficulties as each tries to assert their "professional" credentials.

Our smallest project is one involving Treeton Parish Church and the skills of the local community history group (predominantly ex-miners) working on producing lecterns, embroidered kneelers and exhibition cases in the tradition of church patronage. For me the potentially most exciting project we are currently developing in partnership with Yorkshire Arts and Rotherham's multi-cultural centre is in the field of fashion.

Re-forging relationships that have broken own (including relationship between professionals such as architects and engineers, but particularly relationships between "makers" and communities) is a key element of Rotherham's Cultural Strategy. It is by no means easy, and it is certainly not a "quick fix", but I believe that it is sustainable, legitimate and is far more meaningful to the communities of the borough as we make the link between the past and the future. Using our purchasing power more creatively can make a real difference to our environment, people's aesthetic awareness and to crafts people at no additional cost to the authority.

The importance of crafts should not be articulated separately; crafts development should be managed strategically and holistically. The opportunity offered by cultural strategies to make this happen should not be missed. Crafts must be again integrated into our communities. Rotherham is only at the beginning of implementing its new strategy but I hope you will watch its development - its failures and, hopefully, its successes - with interest.

Commissioning the Crafts - the reality

Paul Swales

In 1988, Sheffield City Council decided it was going to have a Public Art Policy and the then Arts Department, wrote the first public arts policy. The first major project completed under that policy was the refurbishment of the new building for the Ruskin Gallery in Sheffield's city centre. A number of craft commissions were undertaken for this and were received with a great deal of acclaim. They were of course seen in the context of an art gallery, with a collection and a craft gallery, so in that respect, they fitted in with what the city was trying to undertake. When I was appointed as Public Arts Officer in Sheffield, I was asked to develop that policy. This was a brief statement, contained in the draft Unitary Development Plan document stating that Sheffield City Council encourages the commissioning of works of art as part of major developments and the reasons for this are to enliven the environment; to provide community action and to provide employment for the under-used skills of professional artists and makers in the city.

This was challenged by various parties in the early 1990s when we had a public enquiry into the UDP. That information is on the web page which Sheffield Hallam University runs as the Public Art Archive (http://www.shu.ac.uk/services/lc/slidecol/pubart.shtml). One of the great benefits of the city's Cultural Industries Quarter, was that we were able to argue to these objections in that we had a policy which included the employment of artists and makers. The City Council was actively seeking to employ them to develop their skills and to provide some benefit to the economy of Sheffield. We subsequently won the public enquiry, and since then various local authorities have contacted us to ask for advice.

Under this aegis a number of projects have been completed: the Lyceum Theatre, with glasswork by Katrin Jones, is a beautiful piece of work, though very controversial. I was told quite bluntly that we could have bought another lighting board for the theatre if we hadn't commissioned "that glass". In addition, a tapestry was bought with the money left over from another commission. This demonstrates that while we are commissioning work, we're also looking at different ways projects can be undertaken. I think one of the things that we've tried to do in Sheffield is to look and experiment in a fairly serious way, at different ways things can be achieved. This is a benefit to a number of parties, not least the crafts people themselves. It has to be said that doing public art commissions is not appropriate for every artist/craftsperson. Some people do them and get very badly damaged by them and retreat to their workshops, never to darken the door of the environment again. But the important point is that artists and crafts people in a city have a voice in that city, and they can have a way of engaging with the public through public commissions on the street, with collections; with galleries; with community workshops or with schools. These are all programmes which we run in association with our commissions. For example, even the Peace Gardens project involved ten artists working with ten local schools. We held an exhibition at the Ruskin Gallery and all those schools visited, then went away and made things with different artists and crafts people for their own schools.

In 1994, Sheffield Hallam University was building its new campus at Pond Street, below the city centre, and they developed the idea of an artists' team. This was not one of the world's greatest success partnerships known to man but did result in a pair of entrance gates by Amanda King and Chris Twiss.

We do encourage the private sector to commission work. For example, a small lettering project on Steel City House, at the end of Leopold Street. Here, the private sector were asked to do something, they debated long and hard over what they would like to do to the listed building and eventually came up with the idea, that they would like to put the name on it, and we were happy to help them do that.

Another example is in retailing. Sainsburys wanted to do a floor in their new shop, yet somewhere in the process of commissioning this, they ended up with a glass window. A small thing but something where the voice of the maker involved was actually crucial in persuading these architects that they didn't want to do a floor because first of all, you couldn't see it; it was covered in trolleys and the Oil of Ulay lady would probably be standing on it every time you came in and you wouldn't actually see it.

In 1997, we undertook major development in relation to Supertram works. This was a very nice project in that it demonstrated something which is as far removed from policy as you can possibly get. Working within a local authority that promotes public art sounds very grand, but I'm well aware that there are people in my authority, who, first of all, aren't interested, and at another level, may be hostile. This project is a great example of the opposite. The two highway engineers who were detailed to draw up a little sitting area were involved in the commission that Brett Payne did for the Castle Square railings in the city centre and they insisted that we get him back to do a smaller project. They also insisted, when the budget cuts came, that we would change the paving; change the street lights but keep the railings because they recognised that his contribution to this project in the city was the one that people were going to notice and was going to be of the highest quality.

It is not always as positive as this. Mark Veever's planters on Fargate, in terms of experimentation were considering how you might put a number of projects together with different funding packages, and how you might more readily engage silversmiths and jewellers in making work for the public realm. This way not just a change of scale or a change of technique, but the opportunity to work with other people and exchange knowledge and ideas on how objects can relate to the city itself. There were a few of these projects: Maria Hansen's railings outside St. Marie's Cathedral on Norfolk Row, an exemplary project which had to go through the Listed Building process, Conservation Advisory Group, planning permission, Listed Building of Churches, had to go to London to the Church Commissioners and had to go to English Heritage as they were paying for the roof. It took about eight months of going backwards and forwards with drawings, before this project was agreed and the Bishop came and blessed it on completion.

The last project in this series are car park grilles done by silversmith Chris Knight for Sheffield Hallam University's new Stoddart Building. This initiative resulted in Chris Knight making something which is of a scale that he would never normally approach.

To celebrate 700 years of cutlery making in the city we commissioned the Millennium Canteen, for several reasons. Personally, I wanted to do a project where the makers involved in it had absolute total freedom to do what they wanted, untouched by landscape architects or architects, highway engineers or conservation advisory groups or someone who just took against it and was trying to stop it. The joy of this cutlery as a collection of work is it is absolutely superb, and I was very pleased that we actually managed to do it in Sheffield.

This leads me on to another point which is the most asked question I get in terms of commissioning work is *"what has it got to do with Sheffield?"* This question presumes that in some way there is a single identity to which we all aspire to, and we share in Sheffield, and that we can recognise it, and we can touch it, and that is what we are. That's complete nonsense, but it's one that I get asked most regularly. The most recent example of this is the Town Trust project that was won by Shirazeh Houshiary who designed a rather beautiful lead and gold column. I was asked *"what's it got to do with Sheffield?"*, but on the down side of that there was a comment made to me that, somehow if we wanted to do this, instead of siting this sculpture in the city centre, why didn't we stick it down the "arty farty" quarter, because that is where people would enjoy it and understand it. The argument was that what Shirazeh had come up with was not for the ordinary people of Sheffield because they would not understand it and they would not appreciate it and it was far too radical and it wasn't figurative and it wasn't buffer girls. That battle continues and it is one that over the years we have come to recognise and tended to tread more carefully simply because of the political situation.

Amber Hiscott's new stained glass lantern for Sheffield Anglican Cathedral. From the policy and the idea we are engaging the under used skills and talents of artists and makers in the city, encompasses the need to ensure that the survival of old skills in terms of somewhere to work is paramount. Further, as the number of opportunities grows, so the number of different types of work also grows. But, being able to actually make that work and give it a focus and profile is very important. The Persistence Works project for the Yorkshire ArtsSpace group was brought along as their present building is due for demolition. This new building will be a 60 space artists and crafts studio with education facilities and all that entails, notably the marketing of work. All part of the way ensuring there is an economic base for people to work from.

Sheffield is also constructing a new Millennium Gallery, which will house a major exhibition of Sheffield metalware as well as the new home for the Ruskin Gallery. Which brings me to the nearby Peace Gardens project. This was Sheffield' millennium bid and every city had to have one. We decided to completely change the city centre. The key to achieving this was that before we engaged any artists or did any drawings, we did a fairly thorough public consultation, which was done in November 1995. This included a small exhibition of different ideas of what we might do with the Peace Gardens. This project was a bit like messing someone else's front room, as if someone came into your house and said "I think you should move this furniture round and change the wallpaper", and "you don't want that, there" and "have you thought about doing this?". This is the treasured heart of Sheffield City centre, and it had fallen into disrepair and disuse. Reactions to the project were more or less based on memories of the more prosperous 1960s when it was well planted and was well used; it was always sunny and we always won the cup. The city people held a sort of romantic notion about the Peace Gardens. We did have a fairly thorough discussion with the public about this, and collected statistics. The vast majority of people who visited the exhibition were over 50 years of age, which was quite interesting in itself. The greatest idea which got the most votes was floodlighting the Town Hall (82%); grass lawns 82%, herbaceous borders 81%, trees 74%, large amount of seating 71%, and so it goes. When it gets to below 50%, there's a question mark as to whether you should be doing it or not; and then weighing in at 38%, commissioning of public art, fell below the threshold. This information was basically used to draw up the brief for the Peace Gardens so that when we actually went out and talked to artists and makers about becoming involved in this project, we had a fairly clear idea of what we were about, and what we were going to try and do. This was summed up on the brief. The main conclusion from the public consultation was that, a garden is the most cherished use of the Peace Gardens and within that context the creation of an art or craft garden. This had a resonance in the city demonstrating the imaginations and hand based skills of makers and artists, for the enjoyment of future generations.

Once the artists were in place and work was started to be made, in terms of collaboration with our landscape architects and architects, all the artists actually wrote something down. This was done in middle of 1996 and it was interesting to see whether their aspirations, their voice, carried through to the finished product. Brian Asquith talked about Christopher Dresser, our lost designer of Sheffield in some respects, and talked about the industrial background and tools for living, the idea of steel and production smelting, the ideas between the architectural and domestic, and how those might fit together; the association of different types of materials and how they are translated into the public domain. Richard Perry wrote saying "we would like the gardens to engage the people of Sheffield and its visitors by creating a special place to explore, to excite, to have fun in, to rest and to contemplate in". Tracey Heyes wrote "our aspirations are to create a garden that people would want to revisit the soft and hard landscape will create colour and texture that will change to reflect the passing seasons inviting both exploration and use".

You see from these early discussions there was the idea that this is a place not just to sit and relax in but it is also a place to explore. Their ideas and the use of ceramic, stone and steel are evident within the Peace Gardens. Tracey also went on to say the gardens should reflect and celebrate the strong craft and industrial history of the city; we are a city who make things, and people near the city centre are still making silver bowls and plates and cutlery which are being sent all over the world. This is not necessarily a high craft industry in terms of what the Crafts Council or Craft Magazine might show, but people making everyday objects.

As water has powered the tools of manufacture we felt this should feature extensively throughout the site. We envisaged a ribbon of water visiting all areas forming pools and cascading walls of water. It seems to me that the input of the crafts people from the very early stage, (although maybe modified by other design criteria) came through quite strongly as a set of ideas and a set of physical objects that people would enjoy, has carried through the project. Despite the extraordinary long timescale this project has taken, and the amazing flack taken over it, the craftspeoples ideas have remained. We wanted to work with the crafts people selected because of the quality of their work and the quality of their craftsmanship.

Andrew Skelton's bench, demonstrates the thoroughness of the process that we went through. Everything was modelled and viewed before anything was made. This was intensely irritating to people like me who look at a drawing and think "yeh, it's going to look great", but you have to remember that the other 25 people we were working with haven't got a clue what something might look like; of how it might stand up; or how it might fall down; and needed absolute reassurance from everybody involved that what they were making would fit the purpose.

One of the nice things about the Peace Gardens, despite all the policy work and all design discussions, and all the ideas about the post modernism ironic is that this is a place that people do enjoy and that the early ideas that were in those statements written by artists came over very strongly; people do enjoy the gardens. The first photograph shown to our architects about the concept of the pavement, involved fun, a child running through water. A huge battle ensued but in reality people really enjoy the Peace Gardens. People walk around Sheffield city centre taking photographs and if you go in some of the photographic shops they use images of the Peace Gardens to demonstrate the print sizes you can get.

People put money in the water channels. What other craft project have you been involved in where people actually give you money to say well done? They make wishes, and the money all goes to the Lord Mayor's Charity.

I did enjoy the final results of the Peace Gardens, and I hope I haven't painted a dark picture of what we've discovered in Sheffield in terms of people's reactions to artists and makers. I think the commissioning of public art and working with artists and makers is not a short term one off project; it is something which you have to imagine stretches out years in front of you. There are probably times when people like myself should step aside and let somebody else take over, and I am aware that these projects are identified with single individuals and single makers. But, as the message spreads, and people understand what can be done and how it can be done, as long as there are people around of the quality of Brian Asquith and Andrew Skelton, and Tracey Heyes and Richard Perry, and a lot of other people in Sheffield who are getting to grips with how you work with other people and other professions, then a certain amount of work is going to go on in the future. Further, the existence of a new studio building and a new art gallery in the new Ruskin Gallery is going to add up to a fairly healthy start to the new millennium for the visual arts in Sheffield.

The Sheffield Peace Gardens Project

Brian Asquith

As artists we are very thrilled, to have been selected for the Peace Gardens project, and Paul Swales, the Public Arts Officer involved in our early decisions and has helped us through the process from planning to completion.

Our discussions, proposals and ideas for the project were linked with a historical view of Sheffield as a metal working city, involving the use of raw materials, coal, fire, stone and water. The power of water as the source of life inspired the design. It is a celebration of the lost rivers of Sheffield including the Sheaf and the Don, whose waters were essential to the steel industry, and their geographical link to the surrounding landscape of Derbyshire, with its dry stone walls and water sources tumbling down from the moors to the city.

The design puts an emphasis on the dry stone walls and Sheffield Town Hall, the crux of it depending on the horizontal and vertical axis line linking the Town Hall square to the Atrium. The area is both a square and a garden, providing flexibility and access through to Pinstone Street and bus stops.

A garden has been created using water as a poetic element and dramatic atmosphere, an important element that will link "The Heart of the City" projects, Atrium, V & A Gallery, and Tudor Square. The intimate aspects of the garden are provided by the careful and imaginative planting scheme and the installation of contemporary pieces of artwork which give the garden its uniqueness and humanity.

There were three artists working on the project playing an important part in the final design. My contribution was the design of the metalwork and street furniture in granite and bronze, including eight water sources in bronze, seating and bollards, using bronze and granite, planters and litter bins.

Richard Perry was involved as the sculptor to deal with the stonework and had great influence on its shape and form and ultimately executed the decorative carving.

Tracey Heyes was involved in the ceramics for the water rills and the performance area. This included water jets in the paved area designed and selected by Tracey. Her coloured ceramics were also used for the stepped waterfalls and rills. The central performance area, where the water jets come up, had stones selected by Tracey. It was not just a question of selecting them but finding them and piecing them together.

There was a successful collaboration with Rick Bingham. He took my paper design which was to scale and drew it up on CAD which the installers used. I certainly acknowledge Rick's input in preparing the design for final installation.

One of the problems was that the stone work was really very heavy. The plan was massive, and we wanted it to be an industrial place, yet a very pleasant area. The water sources need to have a real presence. I was interested in holding water almost like a cloud. We went through a series of designs: at one time it was going to be in stainless steel but after consideration we worked with bronze, and ultimately we got somewhere near this particular design in which the water could come up the centre .

There was also a very positive collaboration with Craig Bragdy Design Ltd in Denbigh in the production of the water channels. I made the master models at the factory and at my studio, which they then used to cast and repeat. The repeat design was made up of four different units for each of the four designs. During production I visited the factory every week and worked with them on glazed sample tiles. The project was both a learning curve for me and Craig Bragdy Ltd. Despite much experience in making large murals they had little experience in working on large relief pieces, and there were early teething problems the first stages of manufacture.

It was a successful meeting of factory and studio practice. Craig Bragdy were very enthusiastic as it was the first major project in this country and despite early problems in manufacturing we both came to understand and trust in each other's abilities and expert knowledge.

The eight water vessels form the major element in the scheme and are cast in LG3 bronze with polished facets on the top and sides to accentuate the form. Each one delivers water to the cascades and an aerated fountain in the centre of the performance area.

The two large and six small planters were designed in conjunction with the other metal elements within the scheme. The larger bronze elements sit outside the entrance to the Town Hall, cast in LG3 bronze with polished facets on the top while the smaller moveable planters are manufactured in GRP with a Patina finish.

The series of twenty four seats were designed within the elements of the scheme. The emphasis is on a simple structural form utilising bronze and granite to harmonise with the civic constraints of the scheme but convey a sense of lightness and modernity. The base of the seat was designed to work equally well in an inverted form giving more scope for installation. A major group of seats are placed around the perimeter of the gardens with other clusters juxtaposed against sets of bollards. Each seat was cast in LG3 bronze and patinated to match the other elements. They were then blind fixed on site to pre-cast concrete plinths with the granite tops fixed in place by two bronze bolts.

The series of bollards were designed in conjunction with the other metal elements within the scheme. The emphasis is on a simple structural form utilising bronze and polished facets to act as a barrier to vehicles but retain a softness and humanism on the pedestrian interface.

All the time we were working with a group who were pressed for time. I have never done any work or made decisions so quickly. Some of the more adventurous work we weren't allowed, in a sense to pursue, because there wasn't the time to become involved. That we follow through the design process was essential: artists should be there and once you are involved with industry the whole thing becomes real fun.

It was a very exciting project to have been involved in, designing and making such large scale Public Art works - with my artist friends Tracey and Richard.

When water sources were fitted into place, I think Sheffield wondered what on earth had happened. Now all is in place the whole can be viewed as a project which epitomised the creativity of the artist, and the co-operation of craftsmakers.

Brian Asquith, Sheffield Peace Gardens.
© Sheffield Hallam University

The Craftsperson as Public Artist

Andrew Skelton

There is, I feel, something worthwhile about producing work which the public see and use. Although I enjoy working for individual customers, making more and more exquisite and expensive pieces, this is not my aim in pursuing my craft. Working in public spaces and buildings is much more in tune with the original political and romantic notions that first made me take up furniture making. The idea of the carpenter working in and for the community.

I was brought in to the Peace Gardens project in Sheffield when the design stage had been completed and was asked to design within the already decided scheme. I feel very fortunate to have had the opportunity to design and make seats for the Peace Gardens. We tried to make city centre seats that are robust and maintainable but that are comfortable and accessible to the disabled. The seats have cast bronze legs and timber seats and rails – importantly the timber comes from forests owned and sustainably managed by village communities in the Solomon Islands and was imported via a fair trade company.

I would like to explain how we went about this project and, in the light of this, why I feel that the "crafts" – or at least the designer-maker workshop – have a wider role to play particularly in public buildings.

I was commissioned to produce the seats, to an agreed design and budget, and where the seats were made and how that budget was allocated was up to me. From the outset I was keen not just to design and prototype the seat but do most of the actual production. The seats have bronze legs so we made the woodwork and final fettling while the task of casting the legs was sub-contracted. Working on this scale, and choosing a sub-contractor, negotiating, conveying what was required and paying for it, was for me a new and mostly beneficial and enjoyable experience. In my workshop the size of this job (there are eighteen seats in all) gave me the opportunity to grow from just me, to me and one full time and a part time employee during this project, and now to me and two and a half employees, in the hope that we can get some more of this work.

The seat had its beginnings on the drawing board but, most importantly, it was designed and evolved in the workshop. This method suits our idiosyncrasies, our way of working, our machines and equipment. Crafts people are designers and makers, and the sensibility and sensitivity of both disciplines are brought together in what they produce. There is a constant rapport and dialogue, even when using sub-contractors, between what is intended and what is made.

It is by not just designing the seats but by making them, that we have been able to concentrate our efforts where we felt they were most important, and to make our workmanship count.

I do not want to give the impression that I believe that it is only by actually making things that one gives them value, of course the craftsperson as designer is relevant and important. But, we, like many other craft workshops, earn our living by the finished pieces that go out through the door. The dusty, noisy and often physically gruelling daily routine at the bench is at the heart of what we are about.

This making, these skills and equipment, are capable not just of the one off but of small scale production, of not just making but manufacture. The craft workshop as manufacturer or even the group of craft workshops as manufacturer, is not a new idea, or is it a universally appealing idea. But it does take us, as crafts people, past the prestigious entrance hall and one off commission into the guts of the building or development to the architectural metalwork, woodwork, whatever work; to the knives and forks, tables and chairs, the stuff that buildings are crammed with. Behind the one off art work for which we are invited to put forward proposals, is many times the value of work of which we would be equally capable. This is one of the ways of integrating crafts into general culture.

Crafts people welcome public commissions and take them seriously. We can produce on time and to budget. We do what we do with care and professionalism. We are grateful for these opportunities, we need them and we need more of them.

Architect and Craftsman

Peter Clegg

The subject of this talk is the relationship between architect and craftsman as we have experienced it. Through examples of our work, I would like to illustrate our attempts to bridge the divide that has grown up between architects and builders: between people who design and people who make.

Earlier this year, I was in Northern Spain and visited two buildings that were 1000 years apart in age but both spoke eloquently about the necessity of designer and builder working together. The first was the cloister at Santo Domingo de las Casas. It is a Romanesque cloister with exquisitely carved capitals created by craftsmen working within a simple framework. Pairs of columns each terminate in a low relief capital. Set out by the master mason, there is a strict ordering principle but delightful variety in the work of a couple of generations of sculptors.

50 miles and 1000 years away is the Guggenheim Museum in Bilbao where Frank Gehry has again succeeded in unifying both designing and making. Gehry was brought up amongst the expressionist sculptors of Southern California and the building represents a true synthesis of sculpture and architecture, but creativity is also borrowed from other industries. The sculptural forms could not have been made without computer programmes borrowed from the French aerospace industry. The surface of the titanium cladding could not have been developed without the knowledge of the manufacturers working in the rolling mills in Pittsburgh.

Somewhere in-between those two buildings, however, the relationships between architect and craftsman have fallen apart. In England, the divide began in Victorian times. It is symbolised by the image of the "medieval hall" within the Crystal Palace in 1851. Here, A W Pugin put together a display of extraordinary tapestries and beautiful high Church furniture, working with a passionate and religious fervour to reinvent the honesty of medieval craftsmanship. His exhibition took place inside a building that broke new ground in every aspect of engineering of the technology of glass, cast iron and timber. The two traditions represented by Paxton and Pugin were diametrically opposed. The former was a triumph of building construction, pushing technology to the limits. From it grew the great British engineering tradition. Pugin, on the other hand, was the great grandfather of the Arts and Crafts Movement which in its own way tried to re-establish a link between designers and makers, which dissolved into romantic idealism.

In our own work, we feel we owe a debt to both traditions. We enjoy the making of buildings, we enjoy working with crafts people, with part of the construction industry, and we enjoy the creative impulse that can come from introducing artists into the design process. When we were asked to build a theatre for Bedales School in Hampshire, it was imperative that it was built on the tradition of self-build and the use of timber construction. The library at the school, which was built at the height of the Arts and Crafts Movement by Ernest Gimson in 1926, provided us with a precedent, and our challenge was to respond to this tradition and produce a contemporary theatre building.

We were appointed to work with a firm of builders called Carpenter Oak & Woodland and, in a sense, we were brought in as sub-contractors to them. Inevitably, because of the complexities of the process, we ended up as we often do - leading the design team but working very closely with the carpenters. The building has an English oak frame, English douglas fir cladding on the inside and English larch boarding on the outside. It has the quality, integrity and essence of an all timber building. It is a green oak building, i.e. it uses unseasoned oak which is easy to work with before it dries out and hardens with age. The timber also shrinks during this drying process which means that the building itself, for the first few years, moves, settles and adjusts itself. The foyer of the building has traditional frame elements including knee braces, mortice and tenon joints etc. The desk in the foyer is a curved slab of oak that was cut for use as a cruck frame but rejected, and it was good to find a permanent home for it. It sits on a beaten and etched piece of stainless steel.

The main hall of the building uses the oak in a more contemporary way than the foyer. Here, the large spans necessitated the use of stainless steel bracing, cables and fixings that provided a counterpoint to the oak.

The engineer that we worked with, Ian Duncan, and the carpenter's sub-contract designers, enjoyed the process of learning from each other and producing a synthesis between traditional jointing and contemporary engineering.

We also worked with Carpenter Oak & Woodland at The Earth Centre in Doncaster. Our design for the entrance buildings consists of a series of large spaces built into the hillside of the site with a timber and glass building that houses a cafe and information area, but is effectively broken away from the hillside structures. Between the two is an entrance canopy which will be constructed from English roundwood and takes the form of a distorted space frame growing out of tree-like structures and clad in photovoltaic cells. The canopy provides an abstracted notion of a tree, the timber reminiscent of trunk and branches : the photovoltaic cells representative of the leaves which collect and use solar energy.

We also worked at The Earth Centre with Martin Rauch who is an Austrian artist and sculptor who works in earth. He creates installations which are part architectural / part sculptural, such as a cemetery wall which consists of solid rammed earth, no cement, no binding agent, no external finish which utilises different aggregates and textures to form decorative strata in the solid material. Unfortunately, our designs with Martin for the earth wall at The Earth Centre did not proceed, but we look forward to working with him on future projects.

As architects, we have considerable experience of community projects where the involvement of artists has acted as a catalyst in getting the community involved with the design process. One example was a community centre in Basingstoke where there are two installations which involved community participation. Richard Faringdon produced a series of wall-mounted metal sculptures which were translations from plans drawn by children who were involved in the design of the building. Another piece was a stained glass rooflight created by Sasha Ward who worked with a group of elderly people who formed part of the client group, talking to them about colours, light, and the way in which the foyer space could be enlivened.

We designed an area housing office for North Bristol which also involved participation with a local artist, Tracy Hager, who worked with our project architect to produce a series of suspended glass collage sculptures. They were linked to the history of the area and the creation of the building. One was actually produced by a collaboration with our project architect. Quite often, we find that artists and crafts people tend to prefer work on a relatively small scale and it is quite a big jump for them to move to public installations. Here, we overcame the difficulty by suspending a series of glass panels to have a greater impact in the foyer space.

Our work in Yorkshire, as well as The Earth Centre, has also brought us in contact with sculptors and artists. At the Yorkshire Sculpture Park in Wakefield the glass that one looks down onto would reflect the sky and appear like a stream of water running through the landscape. The power of this conceptual idea was strengthened by the intervention of someone whose preoccupation was with light, reflectivity and illusion.

Currently, we are working on the workshops for Yorkshire ArtsSpace in Sheffield. Here, we have been working from the outset with the users who are crafts people. What has emerged is a very simple rational building that is essentially going to provide cheap workspace for impecunious makers. It is a robust simple building, very flexible, and with a low energy consumption. One of the key issues that emerged was dealing with the street elevation which needed to make a statement about the use of the building without creating a "shop window" which would require maintenance of displays. The street elevation has gone through several transformations and we are currently working with a glass craftsman, Geoff Bell, who was appointed as a result of an interview process. We talked to him about the building being constructed out of concrete and asked him to work on an element of glass. He in turn became interested in the concrete itself and is now planning an installation which will use concrete and glass elements set within it. The dialogue, we hope, will provide an innovative synthesis of the two materials.

In conclusion, our work is more challenging and more exciting when you bring into the design process specialist makers. These can be innovative engineers, sub-contractors working in timber or glass, or contractors who specialise in various elements of the building envelope. What the best of them have in common is an understanding of the materials that they use and a creative approach to designing and making as a participatory creative process. Architecture is, after all, a synthesis of design and making.

Production Team, Nazeing Glass
© Trudie Ballantyne

The Craft Maker as Designer: An Agent of Change

Karen Yair

The UK crafts-based manufacturing industries are under threat, facing increasing competition in the shrinking market for traditional tableware and giftware. Lacking flexibility and the resources for investment in new technology, such companies are being forced into a "commodity trap". As retailers increasingly source according to unit cost, they are becoming productivity-led, reducing profit margins and product quality in a drive to undercut competitors.

Although some manufacturers have recognised the need to respond with new products for new markets, introducing change is difficult in a workforce culture centred on efficiency and short-term productivity. Production staff often display a conformity to convention common in times of threat (Tushmann and Nadler 1996), reinforced by piece-work pay systems that penalise any slowing of manufacturing ouput. Design is resented as a disruption, and as source of conflict: designers typically make inappropriate product specifications which lead to manufacturing problems and high rejection rates.

> "The attitude of the factory floor is 'bloody designers'. I hear it all the time. Because they think that, because they make it they're the ones that know about glass, and the designers just come up with these stupid designs that can't be made."

David Royce, Sales Director, Nazeing Glass.

Yet in many respects the post-Fordist economy offers these companies the opportunity to regain competitiveness by capitalising on strengths often neglected in their focus on productivity. Their low tooling costs and flexible production schedules allow customised product solutions, small production runs and just-in-time delivery. Informal internal networks and strong relationships with customers and suppliers potentially provide agility and problem-solving capabilities. In addition, production workers' crafts skills can add value through quality, innovation and individual customisation. Developing these strengths improves manufacturers' capabilities to provide for changing market demands, and for the increasing number of craft makers subcontracting production. It would build competitive advantage based on flexibility, quality, design and customer service, rather than unit cost.

This paper draws on case studies undertaken in the glass and pewter industries (Yair et al 1999a, Yair et al 1999b 1), which describe how two companies are using collaboration with craft makers to instigate change and realise this potential. It identifies the characteristics of a crafts-centred approach to design, comparing it to the companies' experience of working with industrial designers, and describes its impact on both products and new product development.

Craft makers' designs for manufacture are informed by a rich, tacit understanding of materials and processes, developed incrementally through crafts practice. This knowledge encompasses technical information, but is primarily concerned with the material's "feel" - its defining characteristics and response to tools, forming processes, chemicals and heat. The similarities between studio and industrial making processes means that this knowledge is directly transferable to design. Craft makers' work is therefore inherently well suited to manufacturing processes, encapsulating and enhancing the chosen material's natural qualities: the warmth and softness of pewter, for example, or the fine detail and crisp edges characteristic of silver.

In the experience of the two case study companies, industrial designers' proposals are often difficult to manufacture and use, whilst displaying a "forced" quality resulting from the inappropriate demands made of their materials. Designers frequently specify unsuitable shapes, processes unachievable within cost parameters, and a degree of consistency incompatible with available technology.

The craft maker's approach is not only concerned with materials and processes, but is a way of working that permeates the entire design process. Crafts practice is characterised by a dialogue between ideas, materials and processes (Butcher 1998, Johnston 1971). It is an iterative cycle of testing, reflection and refinement, guided by the maker's vision but responsive to the new possibilities revealed through making. Craft makers apply this reflective dialogue to their work with manufacturers: their approach is unique in its engagement with the actual materials of production. Typically visiting the factory early on in the project, they bring an idea to be explored, rather than actual product specifications. Whereas other designers resolve ideas through drawings, CAD modelling and prototyping (Lawson 1990), craft makers work in response to the manufacturing environment, seeing industrial processes as a creative tool rather than a constraint.

> *"We see how it feels and how it looks, because what shows on my drawings isn't necessarily what happens. When it comes to cutting I'll have a pattern worked out, but it might look better if it had 9 repeats to if it had 5. The cutter might say, 'You can't get that line exactly, but if we just twist it like this, then it happens'. Before you know it you've got something that actually isn't very much like the drawing."*

Jane Beebe, glass maker/designer

> *"They take a piece of pewter and bend it a bit, play with it a bit and if it looks interesting then they think, it's a bowl or a vase or whatever."*

Richard Abdy, Product Development Manager, A R Wentworth Ltd.

The craft maker's engagement with manufacturing processes requires co-operation from production staff who are often initially resentful of their intrusion. However, in both companies, craft makers have overcome antagonism by demonstrating their knowledge and passion for materials: asking informed questions; sympathising with problems and showing respect for craft skills. Craft makers prioritise spending time on the factory floor, not only to gain information relating to manufacture, but, also to establish positive working relationships. They use a language which centres on objects, combining words and actions to discuss making and manufacturing. Because this is a language free from professional and class vocabularies, it transcends cultural barriers and enables a degree of integration rare between designers and production staff.

"She seems to communicate a lot more (than other designers). And she doesn't mind being in the factory. She doesn't mind getting her hands dirty. She seems to have quite a good idea of how we go about it, I mean, she ended up telling us what to do."

Bob Garraway, Foreman, Nazeing Glass

The craft maker's knowledge of materials and processes is a basis for developing a personal visual vocabulary. It is a process of informed innovation, where preconceptions are challenged from an informed perspective. Craft makers apply this approach to their work with manufacturers, using their developing understanding of industrial processes to challenge convention. They appear to have the capability to "bend the rules", bringing a fresh perspective which is responsive rather than reactionary, and which sets challenges without making impossible demands.

"What these guys give us is the fact that they turn round and say 'yes you can do this. Because I'm not trained as long as you have been, because I haven't been trained in just one side of working metal like you, look, I can produce this."

Richard Abdy, Product Development Manager, A R Wentworth Ltd

The dialogue which establishes rapport between craft makers and production staff also allows them to work together, synthesising diverse yet complimentary forms of expertise into integrated product solutions.

"Those that take the trouble to work with us and develop things hand in hand seem to be more successful than those who just come up with a design and expect us to make it."

David Royce, Sales Director, Nazeing Glass

This negotiation is rare amongst industrial designers, who, in the companies' experience, typically resist any attempts to "compromise design integrity". However, it is at this stage that new possibilities and unexpected product solutions can be discovered.

"Somebody will say, 'I can't join this to this', but maybe all it takes is me saying, 'well, have you thought of doing this instead?' and they'll say 'good idea' or 'yes, but then there's this that will give us the same effect."

Sarah Jordan, metal and jewellery maker/designer

The crafts-based dialogue explicates "hidden" tacit knowledge that is more easily conveyed through actions than words (Dormer 1998). It produces a stream of tests and prototypes, capturing ideas for future reference (see Leonard-Barton 1991, DiBella et al 1996) and encouraging contributions from others by making the design process visible (see Peters and Waterman 1995). It creates solutions which, because they represent a unique synthesis of expertise, are resistant to imitation by competitors (Rhodes and Carter 1995, Ruekert 1995). In addition, it allows new knowledge to be communicated easily: at Wentworth, this allows development work to be undertaken away from the production line, and the new product "taught" when fully resolved.

Collaborations with craft makers are providing manufacturers with new customers, new products for their own ranges, and new market opportunities. Whilst improving their capabilities to undertake similar subcontracting work, they have given Nazeing access to a lucrative Middle Eastern market and Wentworth the opportunity to target design-conscious retailers. At Wentworth, their contribution to annual turnover has increased from 1.2% in 1989 to over 25% in 1998. At Nazeing, the case documented resulted in multiple repeat orders, product diversification, and productive on-going alliances with both craft maker and retailer.

These quantifiable outcomes represent an underlying strategic gain, resulting directly from craft makers' approach to design through making. Once inflexible, price-oriented and resistant to change, crafts-based manufacturers are now actually developing strengths in product development which could become a way of escaping the commodity trap. Firstly, collaboration is gradually overcoming the resistance to change previously hindering new product development. Perceptions of designers as uncompromising idealists are being challenged by craft makers who respect production staff skills, demonstrate informed interest in their work, and use their advice to inform design. In addition, disruption and loss of earnings is minimised by the inherent suitability for manufacture of craft makers' designs.

Overcoming resistance to change has increased production staff motivation, encouraging co-operation with designers and developing an initiative-led response to manufacturing problems. At Wentworth, it has encouraged certain production staff to develop designs which are now featured in the company's own range. At Nazeing it has fostered a sense of pride that has had a marked effect on both product quality and job satisfaction.

> *"Letting everyone have their say makes them feel that they've made a valid contribution. The ownership of the product shifts onto them, so then they'll take a pride in it and make it beautiful. Because otherwise they won't put that effort in".*

> Jane Beebe, glass maker/designer

In both cases this has had significant effect on company culture, developing the motivation and focus on knowledge-based resources characteristic of the entrepreneurial organisation (see Reich 1991) and essential in developing flexibility (Garvin 1993) and competitiveness (DTI 1998).

A second strategic benefit is in the companies' development of new competencies which increase its responsiveness to customers' demands. At Nazeing this is largely incremental, centred on the introduction of crafts processes such as gold leaf decoration. At Wentworth, it is a pro-active strategy. Product applications have been found for redundant technologies including a steel embedding process, which has been used to strengthen a new bottle stopper, improving its functioning. New competencies have been developed through association with suppliers and craft makers themselves, who have brought expertise in tool making and marketing. Innovative new technologies have also been developed, including a fibreboard encasing technique which expands the vocabulary of shapes available in pewter.

"We can now tackle just about anything. There's no project or no product that scares us too much. There's no job that we'll turn away, and there's actually very few jobs that we fail on."

Richard Abdy, Product Development Manager, A R Wentworth Ltd.

Collaboration is also encouraging crafts-based manufacturers to reassess their methods of managing new product development, and their relationships with clients and suppliers. Both manufacturers are developing the on-going alliances recognised as mutually beneficial in managing design (Jevnaker 1998), prioritising personal contact, service and delivery speed. In addition, they are developing management approaches which accommodate their particular strengths and weaknesses. At Nazeing, a close yet informal networks of specialists provides reliability, responsiveness and resistance to imitation (Rhodes and Carter 1995). At Wentworth, on the other hand, a project team championed by a product development manager focuses allows the conflicting demands of manufacturing and development work to be balanced (Handy 1993).

Finally, collaboration has shown the strategic value of crafts knowledge as a communications tool on an organisational level. Communicating through the crafts-based dialogue stabilises new knowledge whose tacitness prevents encoding in words, allowing it to be improved incrementally through use, recalled easily, and communicated to outsiders and newcomers. This is a crucial strategic role: the incommunicability of tacit knowledge, whilst affording competitive advantage through resistance to imitation by competitors (Edmondson and Moingeon 1996, Spender 1996), can also prevent its application to companies' own core activities (DTI 1998). At Wentworth, the crafts-based dialogue has also become a teaching tool, valuable in disseminating new knowledge throughout the workforce without the distortion that often results from translation into words (Edmondson and Moingeon 1996).

Collaboration brings unique benefits to each manufacturer. At Nazeing, its value lies in an appropriateness for manufacture that introduces new products to a production staff previously antagonistic towards design. At Wentworth however, it also stimulates organisational learning and creativity, instigating a cycle in which collaboration both provides the impetus for innovation, and benefits from it.

> *"They're open-minded and creative, they're willing to try out ideas and different ways that they've never thought of using before. They'll give it a go and see if it works....And they will solve the problem."*

Sarah Jordan, metal and jewellery maker / designer

What is common to both companies is their development of the intangible, knowledge-based resources that underpin competitiveness (DTI 1998), and the development of a new strategic direction based on quality rather than cost. Both are developing competitive advantage through new strengths in responsiveness, flexibility, creativity and customer service that are unmatched by foreign or domestic competitors. Both are offering their clients "packages" of products and services encompassing design, component sourcing, subcontracting, packaging, assembly and trouble-shooting. In this way, both are able to increase profit margins to reflect products' added value and their own unique capabilities. Even basic products can be imbued with value beyond materials and labour, benefiting from the companies' new emphasis on service and flexibility, and from reputations for innovation and quality.

> *"Our belief is that this type of work has got to be the future. These products can command a better price because they are articles of quality and because they have a higher perceived value in the market-place."*

Stephen Abdy, Managing Director, A R Wentworth Ltd.

By creating the impetus for innovation, by explicating and applying existing capabilities, and by creating new competencies, collaboration is re-inventing crafts-based manufacturers as learning organisations, capable of generating unique product solutions resistant to imitation and responding to the demands of changing markets.

Butcher M (1998) " Personal Practice and the Expression of Theoretical Principles in Traditional and Modern Basketmaking" in (ed) Johnson P *Ideas in the Making* Crafts Council, London, UK

Dibella A Nevis EC and Gould JM (1996) "Organizational Learning Style as a Core Capability" in (eds) Moingeon B and Edmondson A *Organizational Learning and Competitive Advantage* Sage, London, UK

Department of Trade and Industry *Our Competitive Future: Building the Knowledge Driven Economy* Stationery Office, London, UK (1998)

Dormer P (1988) *The Art of the Maker* Thames and Hudson, london, UK

Edmondson and Moigneon (1996) "When to Learn How and When to Learn Why: Appropriate Organizational Learning Processes as a Source of Competitive Advantage" in (eds) Moingeon B and Edmondson A *"Organizational Learning and Competitive Advantage"* Sage, London, UK

Garvin DA (1993) "Building a Learning Organization" *Harvard Business Review* pp 78-91 cited in Dibella A Nevis EC and Gould JM (1996) "Organizational Learning Style as a Core Capability" in (eds) Moingeon B and Edmondson A *"Organizational Learning and Competitive Advantage"* Sage, London, UK

Jevnaker B (1998) "Absorbing or Creating Design Ability" in (eds) Bruce M and Jevnaker B *"Management of Design Alliances: Sustaining Competitive Advantage"* John Wiley, Chichester, UK

Johnston E (1971) *Formal Penmanship* Lund Humphries, London, UK

Lawson B (1990) *How Designers Think: The Design Process Demystified* Butterworth-Heinemann, Oxforc UK

Reich R (1991) *"Entrepreneurship Reconsidered: The Team as Hero"* in (eds) Henry J and Walker D "Managing Innovation" OU Press, London, UK

Rhodes E and Carter R (1995) "Emerging Corporate Strategies: Teams and the Changing Role of Design" *Co-Design* no 3 pp 6-13

Ruekert RW (Summer 1995) "Cross-Functional Interactions in Product development and their Impact on project Performance" *Design Management Journal* vol 6 no 3 pp 50-54

Spender JC (1996) "Competitive Advantage From Tacit Knowledge" in (eds) Moingeon B and Edmondson A *Organizational Learning and Competitive Advantage* Sage, London, UK

Tushmann M and Nadler D (1996) "Organizing for Innovation" in (ed) Hart S *New Product Development: A Reader* The Dryden Press, London, UK

Yair K, Press M and Tomes A (1999a: publication forthcoming) "Design Through Making: Crafts Knowledge as a Facilitator to New Product Development" *Design Studies*

Yair K Tomes A and Press M 1999b unpublished paper "Crafting Competitive Advantage: Crafts Knowledge as a Strategic Resource"

I Yair et al (1999a) describes a collaborative project between Nazeing Glass and glass maker / designer Jane Beebe, focusing on analysis of the designer's approach and its impact on company culture. Yair et al (199b) is concerned with pewter manufacturer AR Wentworth's collaborations with craft makers including Sarah Jordan. It discusses the effect of developments in approach to managing collaboration on strategic gain.

The Craftsperson in Education

Kirsty Smart

Northern Artists into Schools *(NAiS)* is a cross regional information and advice agency; supporting artists, schools and organisations in the greater north of England. Currently it serves the Regional Arts Boards (RABs) areas of Yorkshire and Humberside Arts, North West Arts and Northern Arts, covering from North Lincolnshire, the High Peak of Derbyshire and Cheshire up to the Scottish border. *NAiS* was set up in 1995 by the North of England Regional Arts Boards Education Consortium (NERABEC), who recognised the growing importance of partnerships between the arts and the formal education sector. They sought a partner in the Higher Education sector and Sheffield Hallam University (SHU) was awarded the project in 1995.

The project was established to fulfil a variety of roles, which are formalised in different ways within each of the Regional Arts boards. Our aims generally are to be a cross-regional arts-in-education information and advice agency, complementing and linking into existing and emerging initiatives in the greater north of England; and to support a cohesive, significantly influential network in current arts in schools practice, raising the profile of the arts/education relationship. More specifically the project aims to provide a dynamic and proactive interface between professional artists (a term encompassing crafts people) and the formal and informal education sector; and act as an agent, introducing artists to schools according to their requirements. Further, it aims to extend existing networks and collaborations connecting teachers with arts practitioners; to develop coherent and explicit working relationships with relevant agencies and organisations; and to develop our communication and dissemination system to ensure an efficient service to all our users.

NAiS helps to locate school-based work opportunities locally and cross regionally for artists in all disciplines, including performing and visual arts and crafts, puppetry, mime, creative writing and multi-media. Opportunities vary from short performances to six month residencies.

However, the majority of work opportunities, are workshops (sometimes including in service training (INSET) running from one to three days.

There are over 8,000 schools in the greater north of England, a region which comprises of both large urban areas, such as conurbation of Greater Manchester and isolated rural areas as in Cumbria and North Yorkshire. *NAiS* serves all types of educational establishment, from Nursery to Further Education. Increasingly *NAiS* works with other organisations who have existing educational links and who wish to develop education programmes. These include arts venues (galleries, museums), community groups and out-of-school clubs.

Over the last four years we have built up a comprehensive library of information relating to arts and information. This has been drawn from local, regional and national sources such as RABs, funding bodies, research organisations and arts organisations. It also includes a growing number of our own information sheets which have been specifically designed for schools and artists in this context. Recently, *NAiS* was successful in obtaining funding to develop more fully a range of web and paper-based information materials for schools to help them at all stages of organising arts residencies.

NAiS's main function is to help schools and organisations locate suitable artists. It does this through a comprehensive and extensive database of arts practitioners. There are currently over 700 registered practitioners. *NAiS* records information on their art form skills and interests, schools experience, training and qualifications, and details of two referees. When schools request an artist, *NAiS* staff match suitable artists according to the specific criteria provided by the school. *NAiS* does not choose artists for schools, it simply puts them in touch with local practitioners with the relevant skills and experience.

The majority of schools using our services initially have little or no experience in working with professional artists. While there are many local agencies or LEA advisers which can provide specific support in terms of funding and developing projects (for example Leeds Artists in Schools and Bolton, Bury and Rochdale Artists in Schools Programme,) *NAiS* provides a useful starting point. We can refer them to local support agencies as well as provide more general information on developing projects and help locate suitable artists. An increasingly important aspect of our work is feeding this information back to local agencies, and vice versa, to complete the loop. This enables schools to get the best support, and helps *NAiS* build effective working relationships with other organisations and form a clearer picture of arts and education activities across the region.

Artists and crafts people benefit from working in a school environment in a number of ways. Once an artist/craftsperson has built up a reputation, it can be a steady source of income and can lead to long-term relationships with schools. It is an opportunity to share work and ideas and to see how people respond and interact with it in a different setting from, say a studio or gallery. Artists/crafts people enjoy the buzz they get from seeing a child's creativity and imagination sparked, and feel that it informs their own work and helps them constantly question what they are doing. As the arts get more and more sidelined in the curriculum, arts practitioners want to make sure arts subjects are not forgotten about and to feel that they are contributing something valuable to a child's education. In addition, artists/crafts people are keen to promote a positive image and a number of schools have stated that an important aim of bringing into school artists and crafts people is to deconstruct myths about artists and show them as professionals who make their living through making art.

Bringing professional artists/crafts people into schools meets a number of needs from schools' points of view. The benefits which arts in schools bring are currently being explored by the National Foundation for Educational Research in some research commissioned by the Royal Society of Arts (John Harland, Kay Kinder, Jo Haynes, Ian Schagen, The Effects and Effectiveness of Arts Education in Schools: Interim Report 1, (1998) NFER). This research examines the range of effects and outcomes attributed to school-based arts education and what produces these effects. Our own evaluation shows that schools considers such projects as one way of enhancing delivery of the arts curriculum. It can also enhance delivery of other curriculum areas and help pupils develop social and personal skills. Schools evaluations returned to us widely report a strong sense of pride and ownership in arts work produced by pupils with professional artists. Jack Drum Arts worked with children at Cotherstone Primary School in Barnard Castle on a textile wall hanging themed on journeys and special places. When asked why the children thought the hanging was special, comments included:

> *"It's special because it's been made from our minds."*

> *"You feel so important because you did it."*

> *"When I'm a granny I will look at the map and say to my grandchildren: I was there."*

On many occasions Schools have reported how the work has raised the self-esteem of pupils. This was particularly the case at Whinburn pupil Referral Unit in Keighley where artist Alan Pergusey worked with pupils with emotional and behavioural problems to produce cartoonised 3D bird models for a Secret Garden.

However, there is a danger that we lose sight of the importance of developing arts and crafts skills for their own sake. Artists/crafts people working in schools can bring with them specific skills, techniques and ideas which would not otherwise be available to either staff or pupils. This is particularly the case in primary schools where teachers may be non-arts specialists. To be really valuable, an arts project should be the starting point for developing the arts, not just an end in itself. Therefore, INSET can be invaluable in helping staff explore their own creativity. St Joseph's Primary School in Sheffield were such a case, building up their arts department and wanted some professional help in areas where staff lacked confidence. Anna-Mercedes Wear worked with pupils on different types of printing, and the INSET session "helped staff become more imaginative and willing to experiment".

Northcliffe Secondary School invited Brian Holland into school to work with pupils on "alternative self portraits" using clay. Again, staff were keen to give pupils the chance to explore a craft and gain experience with a professional who has expertise staff don't have. Staff were impressed with the originality and high standard of the work. The artist was pleased with pupils' willingness to stay late after school to finish their work.

As the project moves into its third phase, we are exploring new initiatives which support and enhance our core service. The pilot mentor scheme, which enables emerging artists/crafts people to work alongside established artist/practitioners in a school environment, has already proved very useful for many individuals and will hopefully become a more permanent part of our service. With new lottery funds available for out of school clubs and forthcoming results of research out soon on the effects of arts education, it is hoped that pupils will continue to benefit from the expertise and enthusiasm of arts and crafts practitioners.

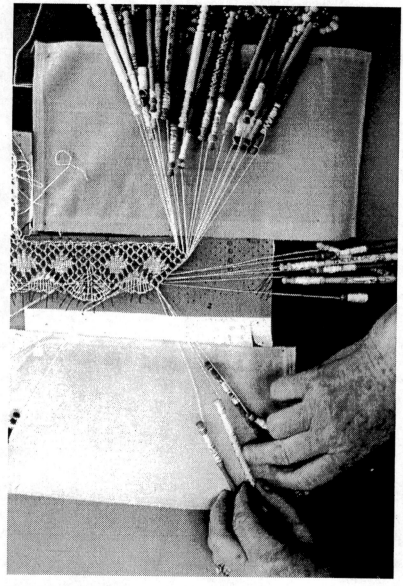

Craftworker Clay Cross Adult Education Centre.
© Simon Nadin

The Crafts and Community: Lifelong Learning

Louise Crawford

In Spring 1998, David Blunkett, Secretary of State for Education and Employment, introduced the Green Paper, The Learning Age. In it, he stressed the importance of lifelong learning in the building of human capital by encouraging creativity, skill and imagination: a good, perhaps even encouraging, place to start.

In its response to the Learning Age, the National Organisation for Adult Learning, suggested that the field of the arts and the encouragement of creativity provided an opportunity for "connectedness in government thinking" in order to realise those aims. NIACE went on to outline the ways in which local adult education services have done in practice to "combine participation in and support of the arts".

Financial security for practising artists and crafts people through part-time teaching; classes to develop good practice; and studies which foster an appreciation of the moral, spiritual and aesthetic challenges of great art.

As the manager of a busy adult education centre in Derbyshire, I could add to that list: The arts and crafts make up a quarter of Derbyshire's adult education curriculum, and we promote high standards of achievement in a diverse range of craft activity. Our largely unaccredited arts and crafts programme puts the student at the centre of the learning activity, motivated and directed on a personal and individual basis. Our tutors lead the field in the practice of community based adult education, and the centre and its programme provide a local focus for cultural identity and activity. The centre is renowned for its friendliness. A good place for adult learners of all backgrounds but especially as a non threatening environment for those who "missed the boat" at school, to gain confidence in returning to education. This centre is as inclusive as it is possible to be. Non judgmental in its efforts to provide space for people to do what they have always wanted to do, and to learn at their own pace.

NIACE has recognised the importance of all of these points in its report in 1998:

> *"The arts have a crucial role in the learning we do to make sense of our lives and to express ourselves fully. Yet such work has been squeezed through the 1990s. It needs encouragement". NIACE,*
>
> *Realising the Learning Age, p6*

So, why has such work been squeezed? And, how may it be encouraged? In terms of craft education being squeezed, the 1992 Further Education Act was a clear and deliberate attempt to ally education and training to the needs of the economy in terms of its number one priority. That is my opinion. I don't necessarily have a problem with that, it is just that education and especially Lifelong Learning is about so much more! It is also my opinion that while the rhetoric of the present government is more than encouraging, exciting even, I remain convinced that the aims of The Learning Age are also rooted in the needs of the economy.

The 1992 Act created an arbitrary split in the adult education curriculum, between vocational and non vocational. The FEFC took care of the nation's training needs and the rest was left to fend for itself within the LEA or private sector. Frankly, arts and crafts education within the LEA did not fare well. The inherent difficulties of precise and systematic evaluation of the existing non vocational arts and crafts curriculum, meant that much of it remained within the remit of cash strapped local authorities. Budgetary demands in Derbyshire at that time, meant that unless a class could be self financing, its continuity was in doubt. The resultant loss of much of the curriculum, ensured that the remainder was broadly only within the reach of the affluent, or survived because popular classes covered their costs. In areas of social deprivation, it would take at least 17 students on means tested benefits to keep a class going. More often than not, they closed.

Whilst Clay Cross was a former coal mining village and has its share of socially deprived electoral wards, much of the surrounding area is not. The mixed economy of its hinterland has ensured the survival of a relatively large programme. Given that 88% of students engaged in arts and crafts at Clay Cross are female, pursuing courses of interest to them, primarily domestic and that two thirds of these students are paying reduced fees, mostly because they are over 60, does not really sit well with an option to accredit the whole programme, if the drive within accreditation is towards gainful employment. Many, if not most of our students have extremely valid educational reasons for not pursuing the "route to employment" model.

In terms of self expression and personal development, the crafts curriculum has much to offer. In terms of "joining the head, the hand, and the heart", perhaps it has no equal, but if we are to pursue these ends within a non vocational framework, let us be clear we must be accountable. One of the reasons we have been "squeezed" has been that within the non vocational programme, we have lacked the framework for systematic, rigorous, qualitative and quantitative analysis of the value of the crafts. Value has been "felt" rather than "proved". It is a fact, and the crafts curriculum has suffered from the subsequent lack of funds.

All that is now behind us. Ofsted and our own Quality Assurance and Curriculum Development mechanisms, now ensure that we work within a framework of accountability, which is as much about recording the students personal gain from the crafts as it is about pursuing the vocational routes of progress. This is encouraging, it is also empowering.

So, what else is to be encouraged? Despite what I have said, accreditation has a place in Lifelong Learning and should be encouraged. I have seen a reluctant group of lacemakers positively blossom within the framework of Open College accreditation. Struggling to keep the group in the face of ever increasing fees, accreditation seemed to be one way of accessing free education as most were on benefits. The paper work was a problem at first, but not the standards needed to achieve the credits. They gained in confidence as they achieved new sets of criteria, much of which they had never dreamed of pursuing before. The accreditation opened doors for them, it took them into another world. For most, it was the first time in their lives that their achievements has ever been recognised on paper. They were proud. I tend to get rather blasé about this kind of thing. It is happening all the time in Lifelong Learning; that is until we have our Awards Evening when it all gets rather emotional as we celebrate our students' achievements.

The National Learning Targets to be achieved by the year 2002, state that 50% of adults should have qualifications to level 3. That is to "A" level, Access to Higher Education standards. That is a tall order, but, if we are to stand any chance of achieving that target, we must look towards learning opportunities at the lower levels; the building blocks of a coherent framework for accreditation which dovetails sensibly into the arts, crafts and design courses of Further and Higher Education.

An adult education centre such as Clay Cross is perfectly situated, both physically and metaphorically, to provide those opportunities and additional guidance and support that working with adult students requires. I, and many of my colleagues in Lifelong Learning have been working hard in recent years to develop the courses through the Open College Network at Entry level and levels 1 and 2 in the arts and crafts. Working in partnership with colleagues in Further Education has been essential in order to identify progression routes, although I have to admit that in my case, dialogue with colleagues in Higher Education has only recently begun.

Something else which should be encouraged is the notion of the crafts within local economic activity. With or without accreditation, many of our students are producing work to a particularly high standard. Our lacemaking achieves national recognition. Much of this work is made for personal of family gain, some of it is not, and is sold at a small but significant profit. Celebration cakes, paintings, pots, clothing and soft furnishing, restoring and recycling furniture, decorating, gardening, all have a value in the market place. Some students have stalls at our annual craft fair to sell their products. Call me a subversive, but I like the idea of local economic sustainability. It should be promoted. I would like to set up a Local Exchange Trading scheme around craft activity at Clay Cross Centre.

Craft activity should be encouraged within projects to promote economic and environmental sustainability. "Economic" and "environmental" are not necessarily notions that sit well with each other, but Professor Mike Press and his colleagues at Sheffield Hallam University have experience of an abundance of craft activities and businesses which do just that. For my part, weighed down by the responsibility for "Human Resource Development" within an economic development project in Clay Cross, his ideas have provided the inspiration necessary to include craft activity within the project alongside the more usual Keyskills and Information Technology courses.

The ultimate aim of the project is to set up a training centre with access to business units and or workshops. It is conceivable that students from Clay Cross Adult Education Centre set up their own businesses in wedding cakes, or make furniture from recycled materials, or it is conceivable that they access HE through accreditation and return to Clay Cross to develop sustainable business in a wide range of crafts and design based activities.

But why wait for a training centre? In partnership with Business Link, we have already started to bring in the "business gurus" to talk to our artists and crafts people about setting up in business. I am reliably informed that third sector employment is going to be big.

Within this project we are also encouraging the status of the crafts within local Employee Development Schemes with small business. When Ford set up its EDAP scheme, providing each employee with a voucher to go on adult education courses of their choice, the company had little indication that productivity, timekeeping, teamwork, creativity, problem solving, perseverance and other "soft skills" would be improved within the workforce. The crafts has a rightful place within this scheme. Similar schemes should be encouraged.

There is much debate these days about strengthening social cohesion, community links and cultural activity. Community based family learning is one way of doing this, and the arts and crafts have a particular relevance with this objective in mind. Of course we have been doing it for years in our adult education centres, but "on the quiet" because our recent funding regimes have made life a little tricky! Now is the time to expand the opportunities for family learning, especially in skills and activities where children and adults can share in the creative, reflective, practical and developmental pleasures of the crafts. With so many exciting skills to choose from, who would ever have thought that learning could be so much fun?

There is of course, always a serious side to fun, and one of our Service objectives is to increase literacy and numeracy provision by 50% by the year 2002. I have used the medium of the crafts to promote literacy and numeracy skills alongside family learning in a bookmaking workshop. It was so much fun that I plan to do more. Other colleagues have been involved in literacy projects which involved making bags and soft toys in the "Books for Babies" and "Storysacks" campaigns. The crafts are inherently important in these projects: they make them accessible and they widen participation. The status of the crafts in such objectives must not just be inherent they must be apparent to the policy makers.

Such a status must be a legitimate end in its own right because a kind of "knowledge hierarchy" in our education system has left its frustrated mark on many of the students I come into contact with. Talking to them about what the arts and crafts means to them I can't tell you the countless times I have heard "I always wanted to do this at school... but I had to do Latin...get a job... showed less promise at Maths...". One of our art tutors, a gifted artist, told me that when he was 16 the careers teacher asked him what he wanted to do with the rest of his life. Glen told him that he "wanted to go to art school". The careers teacher told Glen that he was going down the pit and that a training place had been reserved for him the very next week. After 16 years down the pit, Glen now makes his living from his art and he, like all of our tutors inspire students every week towards their own creativity and to make their own choices. It is what adult community education is about.

Bereavement brought one of our students back to a pottery course. She had been at Brighton College of Art as a mature student in the 1960s. During conversation with her I suggested that it must have been a really exciting time to be involved in the arts. "Oh certainly", she said, "although there was a lot of stuff that these bright young students were doing that I didn't much care for, but I would defend to the death their right to pursue their thing!"

I feel a bit like that about replica Faberge eggs! I don't much care for them but I would defend to the death the students right to make them, sell them, decorate their homes with them, gain national recognition or accreditation for them. It is learning through making.

Of the 1000 students who use our centre every week, nearly two thirds come to be involved in the arts and crafts. 600 people have 600 different reasons for doing so and all of them are right.

Milennium Canteen
© Sheffield Hallam University

Yorkshire Crafts Centre

Alan W. Smith

I am delighted to share with you some excellent news for crafts people in this region: the opening of the four million pound Yorkshire Craft Centre which is planned to officially open in Spring 2000.

The concept began as an idea to form a gallery from some of our redundant textile provision within the School of Art, Design and Textiles, housed in the Lister Building at Bradford and Ilkley Community College. In 1991 we approached the Henry Moore Institute in Leeds for a grant to carry out the initial feasibility study for what was to become the Bradford Gallery.

Robert Hopper, the Director of the Henry Moore Institute was very helpful, he was at that time a member of our Corporation Advisory Committee for Art and Design, he introduced us to a firm of architects, Allen Tod Architecture of The Calls, in Leeds. They had experience of refurbishing industrial buildings and we saw excellent examples of their work such as Square Church, Halifax and The Design Exchange in Bradford. More importantly we liked them and they gave us enormous support in our early vision. The feasibility study was encouraging and we obtained £25,000 from the Henry Moore Foundation. This money, together with the matching funding provided by the College , led to the opening of the Bradford Gallery which in turn became phase one of a more ambitious proposal: The Yorkshire Craft Centre.

The now manager, Vanessa Scarth, was administrating (on a consultancy basis) the exhibition programme for the Bradford Design Exchange and three exhibitions per year over a two year contract in 1992 saw some significant and popular shows of design, art and crafts.

We had considerable support from Yorkshire and Humberside Regional Arts Board under the Chairmanship of Sir Ernest Hall, who has been another inspirational figure for us and continue to get support from the Yorkshire and Humberside Regional Arts Board and the Museums and Galleries Commission.

These were exciting times, but little things stand out, like the moment when Sir Alan Bowness who, whilst visiting us to decide whether or not we should get the initial £25,000 from the Henry Moore Foundation, looked at two pictures on my office wall, leapt up to examine them with the exclamation: "They were done by my father-in-law William Nicholson". I still think that helped to smooth the way.

In October 1995 at a information session on how to secure lottery funding via the Arts Council of England, I found out that as an incorporated (i.e. privatised College), we were eligible to apply for funding. Back in Bradford, the bid writing process began. Actually it wasn't too bad, we were an enthusiastic team, well supported by our advisors, our experience was solid and because we were operating the Bradford Gallery well by then, our track record was good. We were lucky too, because we were in at the beginning, we had a large bid, and were outside London. On 25 October 1996 we were awarded £3,875,00. Yippee!

Then began a long period of tantalising, frustrating and worrying delay as our College Corporation and Directorate went into a cycle of testing the Scheme, whittling down the budget (construction costs were rising) and modifications were introduced. The Arts Council of England were most understanding, and two years elapsed until October 1998 when Balfour Beatty moved on site.

The Crafts Centre itself is a new four storey extension to the School, although some if its workshops are in the Lister Building alongside the new build. At the heart of the Centre is a Cafe-bar and social area with public access to the Internet this acts as a hub between the Crafts Centre, the Bradford Gallery and a third element which is the Bradford Textile Archive, for which the Arts Council of England grant provides us with a shell space of approximately 120 square metres.

This archive encompasses a wide assortment of materials including teaching aids and sample cards, together with examples of experimental and innovative work undertaken by staff and students at the College since the 1870s. In addition, there are also pattern books, correspondence from a local manufacturer, Hind Robinson and the collection of fabrics, originally presented by the Secretary of State for

India to the Bradford Chamber of Commerce in 1868 and subsequently donated to the College. Further donations of materials including seventeen volumes of historic velvet samples donated to us by Denholme Velvets Limited all of which are in remarkable condition given their age.

We now hold one of the largest accessible working textile archives in Europe. This complete collection is to be housed in the specially designated area of The Yorkshire Craft Centre, assisted by sponsorship to £30,000 from the Clothworkers Foundation. We intend operating the Archive as a commercial venture as well as a scholarly repository. Users will search electronically through the material and print up what they need from the catalogued work (which will include images) if they need to see the actual artefact that will also be possible. For this service they will pay a fee of course. This proved a valuable resource for the costume design for BBC *Pride and Prejudice* in 1995.

The Yorkshire Craft Centre has three target groups of users: local people, enthusiasts or amateurs; students and recent graduates and SMEs. It is our intention to offer Fellowships and consultancy, we will advise on business issues, IT and specialist study. There will be workshops, exhibitions, conferences and most of all access to good equipment and fellow designer makers.

We have tried to embody some of our aims within our commissioning plans which, in respect of the Arts Council of England grant, fall into three main categories, a landmark piece being co-ordinated by Urban Fiction, a magnificent stained glass window (9m x 5m) which was a result of a Schools Showcase competition, which is a celebration of British glass manufactured at the Sunderland Glass Company, and a CHEAD competition aimed at students and staff and ex students of UK art and design institutions. This will form the inaugural exhibition which, after touring the UK, will go on to tour Europe. We have a successful Leonardo bid attached to this proposal with partners in Sweden, Finland and Portugal. Yes, European funding will be essential. We have just secured European Regional Development Funding of £465,000 and an ADAPT bid of £70,000 + and intend to seek further support, particularly on the revenue side.

It has to be underlined that without the infrastructure of College support for management, specialists and the whole support staff side, we could not have contemplated this ambition and we are still seeking sponsorship. As yet we have not signed up with any commercial partners although talks are going on about collaborative projects with some key national companies and utilities.

What do we get directly? We get the kudos, the equipment, the manifestation through new and re-furbished premises of our commitment to crafts, the improved access for non-traditional art school users. But, overall, we have a wonderful excitement as we see the interweaving of design, creativity, inspiration and making, coming together on the site of a former textile mill built 100 years ago for educational purposes, which itself had emerged from Bradford manufacturers' in the middle of the 19th Century wanting to put art, design and craft into their production. For good commercial reasons of course, they objected to paying continental textile designers to give enhanced value to their products.

In the School of Art of 1858, the inaugural lecture delivered by William Morris had as its central theme aesthetics and its contribution to the improvement of manufacture. We can echo again today that ambition for art and industry to impact on all of our futures for at least another 100 years in the Yorkshire Craft Centre.

For further information contact:

Vanessa Scarth - Manager
Bradford College Yorkshire Craft Centre and Bradford Gallery Great
Horton Road Bradford BD7 1AY

The Crafts and Community: Higher Education

Andrew Hewitt

Craft counts. Craft is a distinct and intelligent practice and makes a significant contribution to our contemporary visual culture. The crafts enrich the fabric of our environment, and craftmakers have an understanding of materials and processes that can generate business and employment. These statements form the basis of my own practice as a maker and are central to my role as a full time educator on a craft course. The aim of this paper is to discuss how education can attempt to enable crafts students to develop, become versatile, professional practitioners.

I teach at the University of Wolverhampton in glass. Within this subject area we are concerned with ensuring the best possible experience for our students to enable them to develop as makers and to equip them with the most appropriate skills to maintain a career in crafts. We obviously want them to succeed and to have the confidence and attitude to become skilled, self sustaining practitioners. We therefore, have to continually examine the nature of our course by identifying the types of input the students need and find appropriate ways of supporting them. This can be difficult with limited resources and growing numbers of students, but despite this, we attempt to deliver the subject as effectively as we can.

We are a young team of lecturers, all active makers and this has brought an energetic approach to our teaching. We have a diversity and versatility and believe this is an essential trait for contemporary craftmakers.

My own practice reflects this breadth of approach, I work on a variety of design and craft projects, which generally involve glass. I make for exhibitions, competitions and commissions. The importance of expanding my practice enabled me to understand how craftmakers can approach product development and materials research. As a postgraduate at the Royal College of Art, I experimented in combining glass with cement composites in order to make one-off objects and furniture, and subsequently at Sheffield Hallam University I examined the re-use of waste bottle glass as an aggregate in decorative cement based composites.

This led to a research programme was supported by British Glass and the DTI. The project used glass colours, (green, mixed or contaminated) most of which was imported into the UK and excess to the needs of the domestic bottle manufacturing industry. We produced items such as tiling with a highly polished surface called "Homage to Booze".

The questions we posed ourselves were: could we use this so-called waste material in craft and design products and application and could this craft based work lead to the creation of jobs? What followed, were a series of attempts to evaluate the new materials decorative and design potential. The material had to be tested to British Standards and we needed a suitable partner in the commercial development of the process. The research became known as the Metzzo Project a joint venture company was formed with Community Recycling Opportunities Programme (CROP) based in Milton Keynes.

CROP are a community organisation involved with the collection and recycling of domestic waste from the locality. Their aim was to create local sustainable employment. That phase of the project unfortunately ended, due our loss of funding. However, the research did show craft could affect the wider issues of manufacturing and employment.

In the glass and architecture programme at Wolverhampton I am interested in new ways of combining glass craft skill within an architectural context. This can include a wide range of approaches to the material, and glass making processes. We offer a traditional route of working in stained glass and surface decoration, while encouraging an experimental use of kiln-formed, hot cast or blown glass. The approach my be conceptual, decorative, or functional design. The students may use glass either as a vehicle for expressing ideas, or exploiting the materials inherent qualities.

Working with glass in architecture requires the craftmaker to consider themselves as part of a design team. They need to have the professional skills required to collaborate with clients, artists, architects and engineers. I would like to see more craftmakers involved in this collaborative process. Makers can bring new perspectives to a design team: they can articulate ideas visually and understand the subtleties of the material and the complexities of the making process.

There are opportunities for makers using this approach demonstrated in the exhibition *Glass Like Space* held at the Crafts Council. This show was curated by the glass artist Alexander Beleschenko and engineer Tim McFarland. They brought together artists and makers using glass within architecture and selected makers, who fused ideas into exciting resolutions.

To encourage such an approach, the Wolverhampton course includes a live project module, which involves collaborating with local companies or community organisations. We hope this will help students contextualise their work, establish a working methodology and experience managing a live project. The students develop presentation skills (both oral and visual), respond to a brief with their own designs and further their technical understanding of glass making. Furthermore, the students understand the importance of live projects and this generates a lot of excitement in the department.

This year there are three briefs. The first project is working with a local church, to make design proposals for two millennium windows. The church is modern, the brief is for two abstract windows on a theme of water. At the end of the project the students will present work to representatives of the church, the winning design will be made by a student alongside our experienced studio demonstrator. The second project examines the studio cutting and polishing of glass and is linked to a local cut-glass manufacturer and has visiting designers working alongside the students through the project. The final project is in collaboration with a local night club which enjoys a reputation as one of the UKs leading dance venues. Here the students are developing designs for the interior. Their approaches vary from one-off decorative installations to batch produced design for tableware and lighting. So within three projects we have some very diverse things going on.

At postgraduate level, we have a much larger initiative with a West Midlands shopping complex called the Merryhill Centre. The owners of the centre, Chelsfield plc, currently support two students with postgraduate bursaries over a five year collaboration. This collaboration enables the students to develop and make designs for the interior of the complex, and the client to develop site specific projects to enhance the malls, including artworks and installations and create a more varied and interesting environment for visitors. Briefs are developed through discussions between the Merryhill management team, the site architect and staff from the University. The current students working on the project are proposing large scale works and the scale of these projects are both a challenge to both the staff and the students. For example, Nevada Garside is designing a glass clock standing at eight metres high for the end of an avenue of shops. The solar powered clock will become a significant landmark for the centre, with lighting projected onto the glass surface to describe the movement of the time during the day. Nevada's research has been extensive: he has worked closely with lighting specialists, clock engineers and the firm Solarglass who will manufacture and install the clock. The professional experience has been invaluable for Nevada, who now aims to develop a practice of making and designing clocks on a civic as well as a domestic scale.

The second student, Ken Howell, is using the industrial heritage of the Black Country as a basis for his caste glass installation. Ken, working in collaboration with Stuart Crystal, to develop techniques of large scale casting to realise his project. The work describes a legging of canal boats through a tunnels which run near to the Merryhill Centre. We hope projects of this nature will widen the experience of the students by working in live collaborative projects, and we hope they gain confidence in skills which could give them more career choices. Making work for site specific contexts can be a challenging and rewarding part of their practice.

On a more European note, I was impressed by an Italian initiative to bring together young designers, makers and manufacturers. This year I visited Turin to be present at the award ceremony of the competition *Design in Craft Europe*. The aim of this Europe wide competition was for young makers to design work that could be produced by the highly skilled artisan firms in the Piemonte Region which is in north west Italy.

It was anticipated that this collaboration will not only encourage young designers to realise their design proposals, but it would also promote the work of the Piemonte artisans through the accompanying national and international exhibition programme. The artisans recognised the competition from global manufacturing and see new ideas for either product development or marketing from young makers, as being crucial to the long term success of their industries. The competition brief was to design objects, furnishings and home accessories, categories included wood, glass, paper, stone, ceramics, textiles and precious metals. Category winners received cash prizes, but winners and runners-up are now to have their designs made into prototypes by selected artisan firms. These will be then exhibited in Italy, Spain, Holland and the USA, and those winners and runners-up do have some contact with the artisan firms and are actually involved in the process of making the prototypes by fax/email.

To conclude, craft counts. Craft education counts. The nature and context of craft is always developing, and craft education needs to develop to meet these changes. Graduates need to be skilled, versatile and professional in their approach. Craft subjects need to demonstrate both the opportunities and the difficulties that exist for makers in contemporary practice. This, I hope, will enable students to build successful careers in the crafts, and add to the richness of our visual culture.

Fountains: Sheffield Peace Gardens.
© Paul Swales

Craft Citizen

Professor Mike Press

Cities are not God given, cities are not built by investors, cities are not designed by planners, no, cities are made by people. Investors come and go, planners dream and scheme, but when investment goes, when plans which once sparkled on the drawing board turn so sour in reality, what is left is the city: the people and the city they make for themselves. As Sheffield enters the next millennium, its future will be determined not by bankers and politicians, not by planners and architects but, by its people. The inherent creativity and vision of its people. Craft in its widest most culturally relevant sense, is the means of harnessing that creativity and that vision.

Craft provides us with a window into history to understand how Sheffield is made by its people. The industrial foundations of Sheffield were laid by makers, by people who worked with material, by people who discovered new qualities and new possibilities within them. By the very act of making, new knowledge was gained which was to revolutionise our industry and our culture. By understanding and working, with steel, silver, pewter, and Sheffield Plate, whole industries were made - a city was built. In this, Sheffield is not unique: makers like Josiah Wedgwood in the Potteries or Matthew Boulton in the Birmingham metal trades, were pioneers of the Industrial Revolution, combining materials innovation with new production systems and new approaches to marketing. Most significantly, they found ways of meeting the increasing needs of the market by raising, not lowering the quality of their products, and their enterprise linked art and industry.

To put it simply, without the skills of making in engineering, in manufacturing and the arts, there would have been no Industrial Revolution. The material wealth of Britain today stems from that curiosity, from that inventiveness - intelligent making which applies hand and brain in tandem, to understand the world and literally to make a difference to it. And there is something else that *intelligent making* gave us, adult education, the trade union movement, Chartism, a vision of a better world in all the inhuman degradation that the Industrial Revolution brought with it. 150 years ago, half of all the seats on Sheffield Council were held by Chartists. So craft thinking does not just make things. It makes ideas, sees quality in materials and in our way of life, and it seeks to bring about change, as it did 150 years ago and still does today.

We can summarise crafts contribution in just one word: *quality*. The discovery, expression and recognition of quality in the products and the services that we produce, provide and purchase. But above and beyond this, it is quality in how we live and how we work: useful work, not useless toil.

We cannot measure quality, or rank it in those idiotic league tables that now distort our education system; we sense quality. Craft is a form of intelligence and knowledge that uses together: to understand, see and to propose quality. Quality is not something that is discovered by laboratory scientists or identified by focus groups. Quality stems from our intimate relationship with materials and making processes, in the widest senses of those terms. The late David Pye explains this far better than I can.

> *"Good material is a myth, English Walnut is not a good material, most of the tree if leaf mould and firewood, it is only because a workmanlike felling and converting and drying and selection and machining and setting out, cutting and fitting, and assembly and finishing, particularly finishing, that a very small proportion of tree comes to be thought of as good material. Not because a designer has specified English Walnut. Many people seeing a £100 worth of it in a London timber yard would mistake it for rubbish".*

> *David Pye (1969) The Nature and Art of Workmanship*
> *Cambridge University*

So craft gives us a sensibility for quality, for what is worthy of value: it provides materials, products; and in finding value it provides wealth. It also provides value to our cities, by enhancing the public shared environment. Now the idea that the arts and crafts should be seen as a public collective resource is, of course, far from new. Here is another quotation for you:

"We shall enfranchise the artists by giving them our public buildings to work upon, our bridges, our housing estates, our offices, our industrial canteens, our factories, and the municipal buildings where we house our civic activities".

Bevan, Aneurin (1952) In place of fear Gollanz

So, who said that? Tony Blair perhaps, extolling yet again the creative virtues of Cool Britannia. No, those words were written in 1952 by a British politician whose idea of vision went slightly beyond the ten second sound byte and photo opportunity. Aneurin Bevan was a maker, he made the National Health Service, and what few people realise is that Bevan also introduced in the 1948 Local Government Act the first statute that enabled local councils to spend public money on the Arts, and in doing so, he laid the foundations of today's cultural policies, policies that have led to the Sheffield Peace Gardens, to metalworkers creating decorative works for the city centre. Bevan seemed to capture the very idea that the physical health of people is bound up with their cultural, with their aesthetic health - and at the very end of the 20th century that is especially true.

This symposium has provided evidence of craft's contribution to the economy, the environment, education and the culture of this city and the region it is a part of. For most of this century, we have witnessed a dumbing down of craft: a notion that craft is irrelevant, backward looking, anti-industrial, elitist, and just a little bit on the thick side. As we face a new century, craft is perhaps gaining a new confidence and a new relevance. This confidence is to take on some key issues of our time, about urban development, about the environment and about wealth creation. Craft in Britain represents a unique and vital source of knowledge and expertise. It is not old fashioned knowledge, for just as materials and processes constantly change, so too does the knowledge of how to harness them creatively and efficiently. The craft we can develop produces ideas that add value, and quality.

As a manufacturing economy (and let us not forget that we still are a manufacturing economy), craft knowledge can help Britain to compete. But it is not only manufacturers that gain from the value and quality created by craft; the evidence of television adverts and feature films show how Britain's media and film industries are using craftmakers to produce props, sets and animations. That some of the leading digital special effects artists in cinema have a craft background demonstrates how craft thinking and practice is far from rooted in the past. Craft helps give form to the growth industries of tomorrow. We can even see evidence of craft's contribution in specialised fields such as medical physics. One of our Ph.D. students, is making a breakthrough in medical physics in the design of prosthetics. He did a craft course, he is applying craft thinking, knowledge, processes, methods, to research within medical physics.

So, craft thinking has far wider application than the applied arts or industrial design. If the Industrial Revolution came about by makers connecting with their new contexts and meeting the challenges of their age, so too today in the revolution of complexity and radical technological change, craft must reassert a new relevance for itself. Craft as a professional practice, provides us with a knowledge we need to address some key problems of our time. Craft as part of our leisure and learning helps us appreciate the qualities in materials and objects. Craft, as this symposium has demonstrated, has far more value for the world of tomorrow, than the world of yesterday.

Our challenge, must be to take this further, to create stronger, more sustainable links between all those with an interest in craft and creating a vision of how we can literally craft ourselves better cities for the next century.

Vision, is absolutely essential. I recently re-read William Morris's *News from Nowhere* - a wonderful and inspiring utopian book. But how would it be re-written today? Doubtless it would draw on many of the examples features in this symposium. Churches would once again embody community pride, with ex-miners and embroiderers working together to refurbish them. Our older metal-based industries would grow again driven by innovative ideas from craft-based designers. Our city, town and village centres could be re-born as Sheffield's is, in a way that puts people, their cultures and their skills at the centre. Adult education centres could act as a focus for people's enterprise, for people's sense of pride using their learnt skills, and schools could educate children in craft and creativity by working with artists and makers, and perhaps even help to build their own schools.

There are indeed new visions for how we live and how we work in the making in craft. It follows that these visions include re-thinking the role of the maker in tomorrow's city - the craft citizen.

Sheffield Peace Gardens, benches and litter bins.
© Sheffield Hallam University

Sheffield Peace Gardens.
© Paul Swales

Biographies

Professor Elaine Thomas

Currently Chair of CHEAD (Conference for Higher Education in Art and Design) Elaine Thomas was appointed Professor and Director of the School of Cultural Studies, Sheffield Hallam University in 1996. Previously the Dean of Faculty of Art and Design, University of Ulster, her interests range across the humanities. She is a fellow of the CSD and RSA and continues to work as a practising artist. Her work is in collections including the Arts Council of Northern Ireland, Museum of Satire and Humour, Bulgaria and private collections in Great Britain and Eire. She is also a member of the Arts and Humanities Research Board.

Dr. Hilary Cunliffe-Charlesworth

Appointed as a Lecturer in History of Art and Design, Hilary Cunliffe-Charlesworth's research interests include British landscape painting, women designers and the impact of the Royal College of Art on art and design and education. Her first degree was in Fine Art, and she has retained a concern for the importance of art and design in the humanities. Between 1992 and 1995 she was seconded from teaching (0.5) as Harassment Officer for Sheffield Hallam University.

Dr. Linda Moss

Linda Moss was the Head of Arts Access 1988-1990 for the Arts Council of Great Britain, and was the Deputy Chief Executive and Director of Planning at North West Arts Board 1990-1995. After seven years as a senior manager in arts funding she returned to academic life to establish a new MA in Cultural Policy and Management and resume her research in hospital arts on which she has published widely. Between 1979 and 1998 she worked for the Open University and in the Extra Mural Departments of the universities of Glasgow and Southampton.

Professor Nigel Mortimer

Appointed as a Lecturer in Minerals Economics at Sheffield Hallam University in 1985, Nigel Mortimer established the Resources Research Unit in the School of Urban and Regional Studies in 1990. The unit is a full-cost income-generating centre which undertakes research contract and consultancy activities for external clients in the field of natural resource management, specialising in energy. As a consequence of work for the European Commission, he has become the Rapporteur for the "City of the Future" Inter-Sectoral Platform which has contributed to the elaboration of the "City of Tomorrow and Cultural Heritage" Key Action of the forthcoming Fifth Framework Programme. His multi-disciplinary background is reflected in a BSc in Physics from the University of Manchester in 1973 and a PhD in Energy Technology from the Open University in 1977.

Dr. Mirja Kälviäinen

Trained as a clothing designer, she worked as a product designer and pattern cutter in commercial businesses until 1989. She worked for the Finnish Crafts Museum as a researcher and educator. In 1991 she was appointed as the Head of Continuing Education at the Kuopio Academy of Crafts and Design, Finland, becoming the Vice Principal in 1997. She is currently in the UK undertaking post doctoral research.

Jane Glaister

Jane Glaister has been Head of Museums and Arts with Rotherham Metropolitan Borough Council since 1996 where she has led the development of an innovative Cultural Strategy for the area which places cultural activity at the heart of the economic and social regeneration of the Borough's communities. Jane formerly worked as Acting Head of Cultural Services with Calderdale Metropolitan Borough Council. She is a trained museums professional with extensive experience of using contemporary crafts within heritage environments.

Paul Swales

Paul Swales is the Public Art Officer for Sheffield City Council. He is responsible for implementing the City Council's Percent for Art Policy, promoting the public art programme as part of the City Council's environmental schemes and private sector developments. Over 75 public art projects have been completed, with the Heart of the City redevelopment of the Sheffield City Centre being the major project for 1998/99. Since 1995 new methods of working with artists and communities have been explored. These have resulted most recently in the City Centre Metalwork Trail and an education project associated with the City's Millennium project involving pupils and adults. He was the commissioner for the Millennium Canteen, a 76 piece solid silver canteen of cutlery commissioned to celebrate the "700 Years of Cutlery in Sheffield" from 37 members of the Association of British Designer Silversmiths. Current projects include working with the Yorkshire ArtSpace Society on the Persistence Works project: a lottery funded project to build the first new-build studio complex in the United Kingdom.

Brian Asquith

Brian Asquith is one of the select handful of graduates from the Royal College of Art, London, who led a revolution in industrial design and he personally collected six awards from the Design Council. Many of his designs have become well known all over Britain, while his china, glass and cutlery have travelled the world in jumbo jets. He is a Liveryman of the Goldsmith Company, and a Serving Member on the Crafts Council. His silverware is represented in major national collections.

Andrew Skelton

Andrew Skelton studied architecture before setting-up his furniture workshop in Kent 17 years ago, relocating to a remote farm near Bamford 8 years ago. He only works to commission, enjoying both the designing and making of furniture for his clients. The basis of his work is traditional construction in hardwood, though he is always exploring new materials and techniques. He has made work for the National Trust, the John Rylands Library in Manchester as well as the Ruskin Gallery in Sheffield.

Peter Clegg

Peter Clegg was a founding Partner of Feilden Clegg Architects which has just completed 20 years in practice. The firm is known for its environmental approach to architectural design and has been responsible for a number of low energy housing projects, the refurbishment of the new headquarters for Greenpeace UK, and the recent New Environmental Office for the Building Research Establishment at Watford. The practice is also known for its projects in education and the arts and has considerable experience of working with artists and crafts people. Although based in Bath, Feilden Clegg has a number of projects located in Yorkshire. For ten years they have been architects for the Yorkshire Sculpture Park near Wakefield, they are just completing the buildings for the Earth Centre in Doncaster, and working on Persistence Works project for Yorkshire ArtSpace at Sheffield. All these projects have involved collaborations with artists and crafts people. Peter Clegg was educated and has taught in both England and the USA and is currently Visiting Professor of Architecture at Bath University, UK.

Karen Yair

Since graduating in glass design in 1996, Karen has been undertaking doctoral research at Sheffield Hallam University which bridges the fields of crafts and design management. Her interest in the development of new products trough collaboration between craft makers and manufacturers has resulted in contributions to a number of journals and conferences. In addition, she is currently developing an educational video, intended to support undergraduate teaching of design as a negotiative process.

Kirsty Smart

Kirsty Smart took over as the Project Co-ordinator for Northern Artists into Schools in 1997. Her educational background is in music, but her career has been as a freelance arts administrator. She administered several events for the nationally known Sheffield Children's Festival and developed a seminar programme for the Rotherham and Sheffield Dance Project as part of the Stepping Up Art Development Programme. She has worked on research commissioned by Age Concern, England on Arts Provision for Older People and as a researcher and administrator for the innovative Sheffield Live Arts Trust.

Louise Crawford

Originally trained as a teacher, her second subject was ceramics, an interest she has continued up to the present. Since leaving teaching in 1983 she has worked in Community Education, pursuing the "empowerment" model of education through the various mediums within youth work and adult education. Her commitment to the Crafts has informed her professional work and she is currently engaged in looking for ways in which to sustain and develop the status of the Crafts curriculum within Lifelong Learning as a highly relevant, and accountable learning experience for the present and the future. She is the Manager for the Clay Cross Adult Community Education Centre Learning Division, in the former coal field of North East Derbyshire.

Alan W Smith

Alan Smith is the Assistant Principal and Head of School of Art, Design and Textiles, at Bradford and Ilkley Community College, West Yorkshire, a post he has held since 1988. He trained at Goldsmiths College and Hornsey School of Art before working as a freelance graphic and textile designer. Gradually his interest in education expanded and from 1972 he has taught full time. His post as an Educational Advisor to BTEC Design Board provided an enormous breadth of experience dealing with Colleges of Art and Design throughout the United Kingdom. He has enjoyed a high level of industrial liaison with a large number of design and craft operations. He has published on curriculum development and intermediate GNVQ Art, Design and Crafts (1997) for Macmillan/City and Guilds.

Andrew Hewitt

Andrew Hewitt graduated from the Department of Glass and Ceramics at the Royal College of Art in 1992. He is currently Senior Lecturer at the University of Wolverhampton where he heads the Glass in Architecture area. In 1993 he co-initiated a research programme into the use of glass cullet in value added products with Professor Jim Roddis. He is a designer/maker who produces work to commissions. He was invited to participate in the Craftspace Touring Show *Reclaimed Acclaimed* and is currently working on a commission for The British Council Collection.

Professor Mike Press

Mike Press began his career as a systems analyst/programmer for North West Thames Regional Health Authority, London in 1979. In 1982 he undertook research at the Transnational Institute, Amsterdam, and became a Research Associate at the University of Warwick Industrial

Relations Research Unit. In 1988 Mike was a founder and partner of the consultancy: the Research Partnership, Stoke-on-Trent. In 1990 he was appointed senior lecturer in Design Management at Staffordshire University, and joined Sheffield Hallam University as Professor of Design Research in 1995. He is currently steering a European Social Fund "CREATE" project, and is an Editorial Board member of *The Design Journal*.

Sheffield Peace Gardens.
© Paul Swales